DIVINE GUIDANCE

Divine Guidance

The Secret Way to an

Abundant Life

Dr. Jerry D. Overton

Library of Congress Number: 2001118809
ISBN #:   Hardcover   1-4010-3107-2
                 Softcover   1-4010-3106-4

The New International Dictionary of Quotations, Second Edition, selected and annotated by Margaret Minor and Hugh Rawson. A Signet Book. Copyright Hugh Rawson and Margaret Minor, 1986, 1993.

The Torah, The Five Books of Moses, Copyright 1962 by The Jewish Publication Society of America. Philadelphia.

Cover Image: The Holy Trinity by Andrew Rublev, 1411, Tretiakov Gallery, Moscow.

This book was printed in the United States of America.

To order additional copies of this book, contact:
Xlibris Corporation
1-888-7-XLIBRIS
www.Xlibris.com
Orders@Xlibris.com

DEDICATION

*To the Spirit of Love who is gently and lovingly
leading us all to an abundant life—whether we know it or not!*

ACKNOWLEDGEMENTS

*I am deeply grateful for all those throughout my life who have
loved me, nurtured me, and called me forth to fully claim my
preciousness in the eyes of the Beloved.*

*I am thankful for those who so graciously shared their stories
with me, and for the love and assistance of two dear friends:
Anne Grant, for her editorial insights, and Wayne Seeley, for his
help with the cover graphics.*

*And I am especially thankful for the Spirit of Love who faithfully
and continually leads me to an abundant life, filled with joy,
freedom, prosperity, and peace!*

Thanks be to God for such bountiful blessings!

The exact opposite of what is generally believed is often the truth.

—La Bruyere, *Les Caracteres, The New Internatinal Dictionary of Quotations*

We arrive at truth, not by reason only, but also by the heart.

—Pascal, *Pensees, The New International Dictionary of Quotations*

CONTENTS

In the Buddha's later years, after his enlightenment, and after India was ablaze with his wisdom, the people wondered—not who he was, but rather what he was. In the midst of their puzzlement, confounded by his radiance and peaceful presence, they asked him, "Are you a god?"

"No," said the Buddha.

"Are you an angel or some other celestial being?"

"No," said the Buddha.

"Are you a saint?"

"No," he replied.

"Are you some sort of wizard or magician?"

"No."

"Well, then, sir, what are you?"

The Buddha replied, "I am awake."

Traditional Buddhist Story

O give thanks to the Beloved, and open your hearts to
Love.
Awaken! Listen in silence for the
Voice of the Counselor.

. . . You are the Promise of our wholeness,
You await our readiness to choose Life.
Psalm 105, *Psalms for Praying*

PREFACE

SOME PEOPLE EXPERIENCE life as difficult and deficient. Others don't. What makes the difference?

The answer is found in this fact: Our life is usually only as difficult and deficient as we make it. If you find that hard to believe and accept, perhaps a story will help.

Once upon a time, in a land not so very far away from where most of us are, there lived a young Princess whose father, the King, was both wise and wealthy—*and* very generous. The great King loved his precious daughter with all his might, and was willing to give his beloved anything her *heart* desired—anything that would make her life joyful and free. However, the young Princess, having a strong will of her own, chose instead to live in her *head*—and to rationally and logically make her own way. This caused her father a great deal of grief and despair because he wanted only the best for his daughter. But, try as he might to shower her with blessings and share with her the wisdom and guidance necessary to live life with ease and peace, she only ignored and resisted his attempts. She was intent on relying solely on herself, and nobody else. Refusing all assistance from her father, she set out, at the tender age of eighteen, to make her own way in the world.

The last word that was heard about the young Princess was that her life was a complete mess! Her second husband had just left her because of her controlling ways, she was living alone with two young children in a sparse little apartment, working three minimum-wage jobs to the point of exhaustion, struggling as best she could to make ends meet, enslaved by her pride. It was as if she had forgotten that she was a Princess, a precious, beloved, child of a King. It was as if she was completely unaware that she was heir to all that was necessary to live a free, joyful, abundant life—and that all she had to do was accept her inheritance and live it out!

" (

How is it for you? Are you claiming your inheritance—your birthright as a precious child of God? Do you realize that there is guidance—Divine Guidance—available to you that can make your life free, easy, and filled with assurance? Are you keeping yourself open to it in order to get what you need to live an abundant life—one filled with joy, purpose, prosperity, and peace? In short, do you know the secret way to an abundant life?

Or do you find yourself sometimes struggling, feeling uncertain, even stuck? And yet, feeling the need to be self-reliant and self-sufficient, convinced that making life happen is dependent solely upon you, and whatever resources you can muster?

16

Do you usually experience life as fairly simple, safe, and easy, offering endless opportunities for one delightful, joyful experience after another? Or do you experience it as overly complex, fearful, and difficult, as presenting a series of challenges, problems, and crises with which you must constantly deal—all of which keep you from having the life you want—the free and abundant life that is possible for you?

If you find yourself in the latter category, you're not alone. In fact, many, if not most, of us act as if we have forgotten or perhaps never knew the secret to an abundant life. We think that finding our path and living a prosperous life filled with happiness and success is dependent solely on ourselves and our own resources. As a result of our self-reliance, and our sometimes overwhelming need to make things happen, we often get ourselves into some rather trying circumstances. Then, from those experiences, we conclude that life is a difficult and challenging road, filled with uncertainty, fear, and suffering.

The conclusion is understandable, for there is an abundance of evidence for that perception everywhere one looks—newspaper accounts, TV, radio, videos, the Internet. All the various media, even our casual conversations, are filled with the details of one problem, one crisis, one fearful and difficult situation after another—enough, perhaps, to convince us that life *is* difficult—that it's filled with uncertainty and fearful circumstances—and that negotiating it, especially alone, is even more so. Add that viewpoint to personal experience, and one could easily draw such a conclusion.

There are teachings for that perception in some of the world's major religions. The first of The Four Noble Truths taught by Buddha, which came from his own observations as

---

17

to how life was generally lived, is "Life is suffering." Various strains of Christianity also put a great deal of emphasis on the notion of life as suffering. Society in general seems to have adopted that attitude—"no pain, no gain!"

Even various modern-day authorities have espoused the idea in their best-selling books. For example, in 1978, noted psychiatrist M. Scott Peck began *The Road Less Traveled* with this three-word paragraph: "Life is difficult." Apparently those words and that conclusion rang true for thousands of readers, for the book soon became a best seller.

When first I read Peck's book some twenty years ago, those words *seemed* to ring true for me, too, for I was in an unhappy marriage, an unsatisfying career, and was trying as best as I could to parent two young children. And, quite frankly, I didn't have a clue. Not-surprisingly, I felt depressed and overwhelmed. For it seemed I was constantly faced with one problem, one crisis, one calamity after another. My life seemed to be little more than a very hard and rigorous endurance test, a series of difficult lessons to be learned, problems to be solved, and crises to be handled, oftentimes over and over again! I would sometimes find myself gripped with fear and drained of all energy.

Amidst my suffering, I kept asking myself, "Why is life's road so difficult to navigate?" And even though life *did* seem to be just that way, *difficult*, I didn't want to believe it. I kept wondering, hoping, praying, "Why can't life be easier? Why can't it offer more certainty? Why can't it be more fun?"

Peck's answer to those questions was simple and forthright—humanity should accept as fact that life *is* difficult—with difficult problems to be solved. Once we've fully accepted that "fact," then, with a sense of certainty, we can develop the discipline and skills to become effective problem-solvers.

Peck's point was that if we would all just accept as fact that life *is* difficult, then we would not be taken off guard when such difficulties show up in our lives. Rather, armed with a measure of certainty, we could simply meet the difficulties as they come, and begin our task of becoming good and disciplined problem-solvers. This notion fit in quite well with his further belief that it was in the process of meeting and solving problems that we learn, grow, and find life's meaning.

Based on that worldview and that perception of life, I would have to agree with his solution. For if one accepts the perception of life as difficult, then becoming a skilled problem-solver is a wise and proper response. Furthermore, through solving problems we can learn many things, especially how to become very accomplished problem-solvers so that as subsequent and similar problems arise, we can solve them more easily.

And besides, our world values greatly those who can solve life's problems. I'm aware of that fact every time this computer on which I'm typing these words goes on the blink and I have to pay the computer guy to fix my problem. And pay him dearly and even gladly I do—anything to solve the problem!

However, as I read Peck's book, even amidst my suffering, Peck's perception about the nature of life just didn't fit. It didn't ring true for me, for there was an inner knowing within me that felt discomfort with that worldview. And even though life *did*, as I experienced it at that time in my life, seem to be just that way, *difficult*, filled with uncertainty and all sorts of fearful circumstances, I didn't want to believe that it was *intended* to be so.

The thought kept occurring that if life really *was* intended to be precarious and difficult, then it would be but a cruel joke of an uncaring Creator—to subject his or her creatures to such a life. And who would want to believe in that kind of God? What's more, becoming an effective and disciplined problem-solver didn't feel a whole lot easier, or any more reassuring. I was looking for something more!

Scott Peck has not been the only successful author who has put forth the perception of life as difficult, and has made millions on that assertion. For it seems that's precisely what we're ready to hear—in fact, what we *want* to hear! And I suspect that's because it fits with how we often experience our own lives—as difficult. So, it feels good to have yet one more authority confirm what we already believe.

Of course, there's surely nothing wrong with living our lives from that perspective. Being skilled problem-solvers and lesson-learners can be profitable and rewarding ways to structure our time. They're respectable, and, as I alluded to above, lucrative. We can get paid very well for both!

And yet, I still wanted more. I was tired of lessons and problems. I was fed up with trying so hard, living in fear and uncertainty, waiting for the other shoe to drop. I wanted joy! I wanted peace!

It was to take years of even more searching, struggling, and suffering before I could answer those troubling questions for myself. This book is the result of that search and the answers I discovered.

My goal here is to share with you the fruits of that journey—the secret way to an abundant life—and perhaps change your perception about yourself *and* how you experience your life. I want you to know that life *can* be easier and far less fearful and perplexing than most of us have ever imagined. I hope to convince you that although life can be *experienced* as difficult and uncertain, it's not *intended* to be so at all. I will demonstrate that, in reality, life is usually only as difficult, fearful, and uncertain as you and I make it!

Furthermore, I intend to persuade you that, in fact, living a life of abundance—one that is filled with joy, contentment, prosperity, and peace—is really what the Creator intended. And to insure that you can live an abundant life, the Creator provides you constantly with what I've called Divine Guidance, designed and intended to enable you to make the decisions and take the actions necessary to live it in joy and peace.

Your part, then, is as easy as faithfully following the Divine Guidance made available to you. It's just that simple! And it's the intent of this book to fully reveal that secret and show you how.

21

Listen well, O peoples of the earth, to inner promptings of
the Spirit;
Let Silence enter your house that you may hear!
For within your heart Love speaks; not with words of
deceit,
But of spiritual truths to guide you upon the paths of peace.
Do not hide this from your children; teach of the inward
Voice, and help all generations to listen in the Silence,
That they may know the Beloved and be free to follow the
precepts of Love.

Psalm 78, *Psalms for Praying*

INTRODUCTION

I SUSPECT IT would be fair to say that most of us yearn to live an abundant life—one that is free and easy—one that provides certainty—one that offers us the assurance of happiness, fulfillment, prosperity, and peace—all without fear. And yet, for most of us, such a life seems but an impossible dream—or a secret revealed only to the few.

For on a day-to-day basis, we may experience life as anything but happy and fulfilling, free and easy. All too often we find ourselves living out our fear and uncertainties—scurrying about, trying to make ends meet, keep the relationship together, pay the bills, tend to the children, do our jobs well enough to keep from getting fired or replaced by someone younger or more aggressive, do the household chores, find a moment for ourselves, and on and on and on—until finally we're able to collapse into bed only to have to rise all too soon and do it all over again!

Even if we do find a moment to self-reflect, and do decide that this is *not* the life we want, we may find ourselves perplexed and confused because we don't have a clue as to what such a happy, fulfilling, free and easy life would even look like—much less how to have it. It all feels so uncertain! And it's then, in the midst of our uncertainties, that we may find out how quickly we can slide down that slippery slope of depression—at least the low-grade type—in which we can easily conclude what we've feared all along, that perhaps it doesn't really get any better than we've got it!

I find this to be the case often in my practice as a Personal Coach. Many people don't have any idea how to have the life they want, or what that life would entail. They're not sure it's even possible. All they know is that they have this nagging sense of unhappiness, and uncertainty and fear are lurking everywhere. And they've finally concluded that they can't seem to get out of the slump on their own.

It's with these folks that I can start to rejoice. For it's precisely at this critical point in their lives that they have the best shot at getting the guidance they need, because in the midst of their uncertainty, they *know* they need help.

To them, and to you if any of this fits, I pose these questions: What if there was a way that you could be *assured* of having an abundant life? What if you didn't have to try so hard and feel so vulnerable as you attempt to make the right decisions and find the right path for you? What if discovering and leading a happy, fulfilling, prosperous life was not intended to be difficult or fearful at all? What if it was really intended to be easy—as easy as reading and following a source of information—guidance—so reliable that you could be assured of easily and confidently making the decisions necessary to create the life you want, and avoid most all the pitfalls, dangers, trials, and crises as you do so?

This book is intended to give you the secret—to present you with the convincing evidence that having the life you want *can* be just that certain—that simple and easy—as certain, simple, and easy as learning to read, trust, and follow the Divine Guidance of God that is constantly being made available to you. And that as you begin to do so, you can avoid most of life's difficulties as you discover and live the life of your dreams with certainty, in joy, abundance, and peace!

Sounds too good to be true, you say? Then, please, hear me out.

I base such a notion on the faithful belief that we are created not as individuals who are left to constantly fend for ourselves as we try to find our own way through the maze of life, but rather as a precious and integral part of a larger created order. As part of this larger whole, the Creator God, out of great and gracious love for all of creation, makes Divine Guidance available to each of us to fulfill God's will for us to live in joyful harmony and peace with all of creation.

It is this same God of the Universe who serves not only as the Source of the Divine Guidance we need to show us the way to a happy, fulfilling, and peaceful life, but Who actually presents it to us several different times, in several different ways, and in increasing degrees and intensities, in order to finally attract our attention and have us "get it" so we can then live it. As we live by God's Divine Guidance, then we can know with assurance the abundant life of joy, prosperity, and peace for which we yearn.

According to my own personal experience, as well as my observation and experience of others, I am convinced that

25

the God of the Universe provides at least six different types of Divine Guidance for us to use in order to have the abundant life God wills for us. These six types fall into two basic categories.

The first category, described in depth in Part II of this book, "Direct Divine Guidance," includes the three basic types of Direct Divine Guidance that God provides as God seeks to lead us to a peaceful, joyful, and abundant life. These include inklings, nudges, and messages.

The second category, described in Part III, "Divine Guidance Through the Consequences," includes the continued guidance that God gives to us even when we have failed to heed, for whatever reason, the Direct Divine Guidance, and have found ourselves off track and dealing with the resulting difficult and natural consequences. I've grouped these resulting consequences under the three general categories of lessons, problems, and crises. My point here is that when we haven't heeded the direct guidance from God and are dealing with one of these natural consequences, then God can and does use the consequences to bring us to conscious awareness of the continued direct guidance that God is giving to us so that we can benefit from it and avoid further consequences.

As God persists in seeking to give us directly the Divine Guidance we need, God may make use of any of the three types of Direct Divine Guidance, the inklings, nudges, and messages, using a certain sense of urgency and persistency, until we get it. What this means is that as we choose, either consciously or unconsciously, to ignore the Divine Guidance made available to us, God, out of God's unceasing, unconditional love and care for us, as well as God's intention to maintain harmony throughout the created order, will try again. God will first use the direct guidance. When that fails to get through to us, and we find ourselves dealing with lessons, problems, and crises, God will work through these inevitable consequences, using them as means to "wake us up" so that then we might still get the guidance we need.

Within the first category, that of Direct Divine Guidance, each new effort may bring an increased intensity in the attempt. If we don't get it with inklings, if we don't pay attention and act on the guidance given, then we may experience a second type of guidance, nudges, which are stronger, more intense, and more obvious. If we still don't get it, God may make use of a third attempt, that of messages, which may be still more obvious and even more tangible.

It's much like the clock radio I use to awaken me in the mornings. It has two different alarms, one I can set for soft music, and one for a loud buzzer. If the first one doesn't get me up and about with its soft approach, then the second, more intrusive, one will, or at least has a more intense shot at it!

Even though we may fail to get the guidance we need directly, and thus find ourselves neck-deep in the inevitable consequences that can come as we get off course, including the aforementioned lessons, problems, and crises, God doesn't stop trying to give us the guidance that will keep life simple, easy, fun, and abundant. On the contrary, God continues to send forth the guidance, now by offering it through the consequences themselves.

It works like this. When we follow the Divine Guidance, we can avoid most of life's difficulties and live our life free from fear, in joy and peace. When we fail to get the guidance directly, we are vulnerable to and may have to suffer through or at least deal with these resultant consequences—the lessons, problems, and crises. However, rather than give up on us as a lost cause, God takes a new tack and makes use of what is at hand—whatever consequences in which we may find ourselves. God uses these consequences—these lessons, problems, and crises—as a sort of second "wake up call"—like the buzzer on my alarm—to get our lives back on track. The intensity of the consequence can serve as the "alarm" we may need to help us "wake up" and "hear" and thus be able to heed the guidance as it now comes. I'll say much more about how this works in Part III.

As you can see, it is to our direct advantage to "get it" as soon as possible so that we may avoid as many of these difficult consequences as possible! For the sooner we get the Divine Guidance we need, the sooner we can make use of it. And the sooner we make use of it, the easier our life is and the more effective and joyful our journey because we have avoided the increasingly severe natural consequences. Also, the more harmony will exist within the created order!

Unfortunately, most of us have been conditioned out of our innate ability to read and trust this divine language of God, especially as it is given to us directly. As children, this ability came very naturally to us, but as we matured we were taught, directly or indirectly, consciously or unconsciously, to ignore and distrust such Divine Guidance.

Instead, we were taught to trust more fully in ourselves, in our five senses, and in our intellectual and rational minds to carefully gather information from various sources, sift through it, and then make a rational decision as to what we should do in every situation. "Think for yourself!" we were told, and soon we did! And soon we no longer heard or trusted the Divine Guidance that was still being given to us. Rather, we looked to ourselves.

To be sure, there is nothing innately wrong with such an approach. In fact, for most of us, the practice of looking to ourselves for the information we've needed to negotiate life has worked, and has done so fairly well and often. For most of us, it is our way of life. It's the only way we know.

And yet, for most of us, this approach has also come at great personal expense, emotionally, physically, spiritually, and mentally, as we have missed the Divine Guidance and then had to suffer through the resulting consequences. As a result of relying only on ourselves, we've been confronted with and have had to endure these consequences over and over again. We've learned and re-learned more lessons, struggled with and suffered through more problems, and survived, sometimes by the skin of our teeth, more crises than we care to remember. And our experiences with these natural consequences have instilled in us a great deal of fear and trembling, much anxiety, and a large measure of self-doubt and uncertainty. It's made life seem fearful and difficult at best. And sometimes the uncertainties have made it all but unbearable!

One of the obvious costs to us, when we rely solely on ourselves, is that it usually takes us an inordinate amount of time, energy, and resources, not to mention the stress involved, to gather the data, sort through it, and make our decisions about how best to live our life. Consider the number of file cabinets we cram full of information, just *in case* (no pun intended) we need it, though we rarely do, not to mention the multi-gigabytes of data we compress onto our computer hard drives and link together in web sites! That in itself would be reason enough for most of us to seek a better way, or at least to question a creator who would leave its creatures with such a precarious and costly way to negotiate their world!

Sometimes, as we consider a better way, we may think that means relying on those about us—our spouses, friends, children, parents, colleagues, pastors, and others. And yet, when we choose to rely on them, we can sometimes multiply the cost factor, especially with regards to the levels of uncertainty, vulnerability, and stress we encounter. For when we look to others, we put ourselves at their disposal, on their timetable, and dependant on their knowledge, energy, interest, and resources—not to mention their mental health, their motives to help, and any vested interests they may have. That can all be rather precarious for us, depending on how willing and able they are to give us the accurate and unbiased information we need to live our lives.

The point I'm trying to make here is that instead of relying on ourselves or even those about us for the guidance we need to negotiate life, the better way is to rely on God's Divine Guidance, basically because it works! I hope to make that point obvious as you proceed through this book.

However, at this juncture a question may be formulating in your mind. You may be asking, "If it's true that the better way *is* to rely on God's Divine Guidance to enable us to live a joyful, abundant, and peaceful life, then why haven't we made better use of it?"

There are many logical reasons why we haven't and/or don't make use of Divine Guidance. I'll suggest a few.

Perhaps the first, most obvious, reason is that many, if not most, of us were never made aware of the existence of Divine Guidance. This includes our primary caretakers, usually our mothers and fathers, who would have been the likely sources of such knowledge. Instead, we received what is often referred to as "good parenting." Without the benefit of the knowledge of Divine Guidance, our parents saw it as *their* responsibility, even their duty, to take care of us. In so doing, they made us dependent on *them* for our well-being. We were taught to look to them, and often them alone, for what we needed to grow up and learn to successfully negotiate our world.

Then, when they felt we were old enough and mature enough, they often sought to transfer that responsibility to us. The plan was that as we became knowledgeable enough and responsible enough as young adults, we were supposed to take care of ourselves. We were to rely on our own abilities, knowledge, resources, and skills to negotiate life. Or, we were to look to others whom we considered capable, reliable, and trustworthy, especially our spouse or life partner, to help us do it—which may be why many parents encourage their children to marry as soon as possible!

In this way of parenting, we were never taught to look to Divine Guidance. Because many parents didn't know anything about it, we didn't either. Or if they did know something about it, it was often suspect, and we, then, were discouraged from acknowledging or trusting it. For it was usually misunderstood or seen as but a child's fantasy, as immature, irrational, and therefore untrustworthy.

Another reason we haven't made use of Divine Guidance is because our various other "teachers," including those to whom we might have looked for such knowledge in spiritual affairs, like our pastors or church school teachers, didn't know anything about Divine Guidance either. Because they had never been taught it, they couldn't teach us. And thus we grew up with no skills to "hear" or "see" the Divine Guidance. Then, because we couldn't "receive" it, we couldn't use it.

31

Or perhaps we did have some awareness of it, but because we weren't encouraged to trust it or use it, we didn't. After all, it wasn't seen to be very "rational" or "tangible." Therefore, it couldn't be acknowledged or trusted. So slowly, as we "matured," we lost all ability to receive it.

For some, it was a matter of never having been taught the skills of discernment—how to decide what was truly Divine Guidance and what was just the chatter in their heads. So, they ignored it all.

For others, especially those in certain more fundamental religious circles, the guidance was often misunderstood and misinterpreted, seen as but human impulses, and was often distrusted. Sometimes it was thought to be demonic, or at least seen as subtle forms of "temptation" designed to get one off course. Such ones were taught to disregard or even actively fight against following these human "impulses." Instead, they were to look only to their own religious teachings or to scripture for the guidance they needed to live life.

Still others have found it too hard to believe, or perhaps too good to be true, that God would actually be present to them and offer them any sort of personal guidance. Their doubt and disbelief has stood in their way.

For some, it's just a matter of being too busy to hear. They're going at ninety-to-nothing all the time and never stop their busyness long enough to listen or pay attention. Their heads are filled with the buzz and chatter of all their activity, and they probably couldn't hear even if they were willing, or at least until they were willing to slow down long enough to still the roar.

For a vast number of people, because they live in what can only be described as a low-grade depression, they are just too tired, too stuck, too fragile, or too scared to learn or make use of Divine Guidance. They're doing all they can do to put one foot in front of the other, to keep their jobs intact, to pay the mortgage, and to keep it all together to do one more thing. For these folks, and I believe there are tens of millions of them out there, I find myself having a great deal of compassion. For I know, personally, what that's like, and I know that it is precisely Divine Guidance that could lift them out of their depression, as it has me, get them engaged in life, and give them joy again.

As you can see, there are many reasons why we either can't or won't make use of Divine Guidance. Because it is not within the scope of this book to go into all the reasons why and how most of us have been conditioned out of our natural ability to read and trust the Divine Guidance of the God of the Universe, suffice it to say that most of us have. I leave it to you to figure out just how it may have happened to you! I will, however, continue to give some clues as we go along as to how it might have happened, which may also help you in reclaiming your natural abilities.

What *is* within this book's scope is to introduce at least six ways that the God of the Universe attempts to present to us necessary information through Divine Guidance. Each way has the intent to wake us up to the particular guidance that God has for us—guidance that we will need and can use to live free, happy, and abundant lives.

Our part then, as ones who want to make use of this Divine Guidance, is twofold. First, to simply trust that, indeed, God does have and constantly offers to us Divine Guidance that will lead us to a joyful and prosperous life. And secondly,

33

to develop our senses, our intuition, our skills, and our level of trust to the point that we can read the language, get the guidance, and follow its course.

To do our part requires that we must also be willing to give up our old, "tried and true" ways that have served us through the years, albeit ever so costly, precariously, and painfully at times. This may be no easy task for us, for we have been carefully taught and have grown to trust the old process and the old sources, even though they have failed us on many occasions, and left us feeling vulnerable, and oftentimes rather hopeless and in despair. However, as we do begin to trust this "new," although old-as-time, way of Divine Guidance, we may soon discover just how trustworthy it is, and how certain we can become of its effectiveness. And we may find ourselves growing increasingly adept at making use of its guidance, and beginning to know freedom and ease like we've never imagined!

To begin getting the Divine Guidance we need from God, all that's really required is for each of us to have a willingness to trust and give it a try! The great and gracious God of the Universe will take care of the rest.

In the chapters that follow, you will be given some necessary understandings that will make it possible for you to re-decide your perception of yourself and the nature of life, and follow the Divine Guidance. You will find described and illustrated six ways God seeks to offer us the Divine Guidance we need for a free, happy, and abundant life. You will also find illustrative anecdotes as to how others have received the Guidance, even though often unawares until later reflective hindsight or until pointed out to them by someone else. You will see how they either made use of the guidance or did not, and the consequences of each response.

In each case you will be invited to think of examples in your own life when Divine Guidance was made available to you, and whether or not you acknowledged and made us of it at the time. And in each case, skills will be offered that can help you be able to recognize such guidance even as it is being offered to you, so that you may begin to make use of it more quickly, with much less pain and suffering, and far more effectiveness.

I will then conclude by building what I hope is a strong case for a much better way of living our lives—a way that is much less fearful and far more easy than the old ways to which most may be accustomed—a way that will insure that we live an abundant life. I will show that it's simply not necessary for us to continue to live in fear and uncertainty as we spend our time learning the same repetitive lessons over and over again, suffering through and hoping to solve the constant barrage of problems, and encountering and hoping to outlive the series of crises that come at us. This better way is by simply making routine use of this trustworthy source of Divine Guidance provided by the God of the Universe for the purpose of insuring us a peaceful path to an abundant life.

I offer this because, personally, I've struggled long enough and failed far too often to get the guidance I've needed as I've relied solely on my own resourcefulness or that of others, and I suspect you have, too. And I'm sure you would agree, it's just not much fun, unless you're really into lots of pain and suffering! Therefore, I'd like to see you spared such needless self-abuse.

For the fact of the matter is that there *is* a better way! And it's time you knew more about it and made use of it.

DR. JERRY D. OVERTON

My hope is that through what is offered here, you may either begin or continue to deepen your trust in the God of the Universe as a Source of perfect Divine Guidance for you, and that you may develop and use the skills necessary to get the guidance you need to live a free, happy, and abundant life. You deserve nothing less!

For there really is a better way for you to live your life—a practical, peaceful way to a prosperous, abundant life. May you find the secret in these pages and live in joy and bliss!

Trust in the Lord with all your heart, on your own intelligence rely not;
In all your ways be mindful of him, and he will make straight your paths.

Proverbs 3:5-6, *New American Bible*

Part I

Necessary Understandings

In order for you to best use this book to fully learn the secret that will enable you to live a divinely guided, abundant life, certain basic understandings are necessary. In Part I, I will share the basis and intent of this book so that you will get a clear picture of where we're headed. I will share with you the two commonly held worldviews that determine, to a large extent, one's experience of life. I will set forth three notions of the nature of humanity that will help describe why most people find it so difficult to live an abundant life. And I will share my basic underlying principle, and how that principle, if followed, can insure that each of us lives the abundant life that awaits us.

May you find these understandings helpful. May they give you pause to examine your own perceptions, and re-decide them as necessary. And may you use these understandings to find the secret way to a prosperous life.

.

NECESSARY UNDERSTANDINGS

The Basis and Intent of the Book

IT WAS PIERRE Teillhard de Chardin who put it best when he wrote: "We are not human beings having a spiritual experience. We are spiritual beings having a human experience."

With that in mind, my over-all intent in this book is two-fold. First, to demonstrate to you that as a spiritual being, to have a human experience is not intended to be fearful and difficult at all. Rather it is intended to be joyful and easy, primarily because there *is* guidance, Divine Guidance, available to you. And that as you learn to read, trust, and follow this Divine Guidance, it will lead you into a life of abundance and peace.

And secondly, to show you that if you will but follow the Divine Guidance available to you, then not only will you have the life just described, you can also avoid most of life's uncertainty and its fearful difficulties—its lessons, problems, and crises—its trials and tribulations, its pain and suffering—and your life will be much easier and far more fun, fulfilling, and peaceful.

I know that at this point you may be thinking that this seems pretty far-fetched, unrealistic, naive, and even pie-in-the-sky. I understand. Believe me, I do. For there was a period in my life, a very long and extended period, when in the midst of my own fear, pain, and struggles I felt the same way. So, give me a few more minutes and at least hear me out.

In order to build my case, this book takes as true the following beliefs. First, that we are indeed spiritual beings having a human experience. Although we do live in a body, and have to meet the needs of our bodies, we are still spiritual beings.

Secondly, that as spiritual beings, there lives within us a Divine Spirit of Love, the very Spirit of God. Some call this Spirit their Higher Power, their Source, the Divine Spark, the Holy Spirit, the Creator, or simply God. This Divine Spirit loves us unconditionally and seeks constantly to give us the guidance we need to live life in our humanity freely, easily, and abundantly, with joy and peace.

Thirdly, all that you or any of us has to do to have such a happy, abundant, divinely guided life is to learn to recognize, read, and then follow the signs provided. We're not left merely to the uncertainty of our own intellect or resources. We have constant access to the trustworthy guidance of the Divine Spirit.

Fourthly, when, for whatever reason, we do *not* make use

of the Divine Guidance, we will probably wind up having to deal with certain difficulties which come as natural consequences of our actions. These difficulties usually are a natural result of relying on ourselves to make our decisions rather than making use of the Divine Guidance, and include such things as repetitive lessons, complicated problems, and death-dealing crises.

And fifthly, even when we do overlook or ignore the Divine Guidance and find ourselves stuck and struggling with one of those consequences, God does not give up on trying to provide us with the guidance we need. Rather, God is still there to work through that difficulty—that lesson, problem, or crisis—and even make use of it to wake us up to the Divine Guidance available to us to help us live life with joy and peace.

Based on these beliefs which I hold to be true, the question then becomes, "If this is so, are you willing and able to do it? Are you both willing and able to follow this Divine Guidance in order to have the life of your dreams?"

In order to prepare you to best answer that question in the affirmative, the intent of this book is fourfold. First, to confirm and hopefully convince you that as a spiritual being, there is within you the Power and Wisdom of God who is constantly seeking to give you the Divine Guidance you need to a live happy, productive, meaningful, and abundant human life.

Secondly, to give you the knowledge and awareness you need to recognize and see this Divine Guidance as it comes.

Thirdly, to teach you the skills to follow the Divine Guidance given so that you can live in joy, peace, and abundance.

And fourthly, to present you with enough convincing evidence, both from my own experience and that of others, that will enable you to be willing to trust and follow the Divine Guidance as it is given to you.

That will be my part in this process—to convince you that you are *able* to follow the guidance. Your part, then, is to decide you are *willing*. For in order for you to have such a divinely guided life, you must come to believe that Divine Guidance *is* being made available to you, that it is trustworthy, and that if you follow it then it *will* lead you to a life of joy and peace. And, you must learn to recognize, understand, and follow the Divine Guidance given to you. For I am convinced that if you do, then you can radically change your experience of life, and more readily and more fully live it with joy, abundance, and peace.

God, whose love and joy are present everywhere, can't come to visit you unless you aren't there.

—Angelus Silesius (1624-1677), *The Enlightened Heart*

NECESSARY UNDERSTANDINGS

The Two Worldviews

IN ORDER FOR us to live an abundant life, perhaps the first thing we must do is acknowledge and address our basic worldview—our perception of life. As we change our perception, we can change our life.

What I've discovered over the years is that there are at least two worldviews—two possible perceptions—that influence and determine how you will experience life. Therefore, the nature and quality of your life is determined by which worldview you believe to be true.

One worldview, the perception alluded to above, is that life *is* difficult and filled with fearful challenges—and is intended to be so. Under this world view, the conclusion is that in order to successfully negotiate life, and to learn, grow, and find meaning and purpose, we must first accept that life *is* that way, and then do all we can to become effective and courageous managers of the expected difficulties. And the most obvious way to do that is to become very skilled problem-solvers, lesson-learners, and crisis-survivors.

Proponents of this worldview have put forth volumes of materials on how best to become accomplished managers of life-as-difficult. Go into any bookstore and the shelves are lined with self-help books teaching various methods and strategies for becoming good problem-solvers, lessons-learners, and crisis-survivors. Readers buy them like hot cakes, and they do so for at least two reasons. First, because they are all but terrified and are desperate to handle what they believe are the necessary and expected difficulties of life and move through them as unscathed as possible. And secondly, and perhaps more importantly, they hope that as they work and move through these difficulties, they might grow more toward wholeness—toward the joy and peace they crave.

Those who hold to this worldview tend to hold to the necessity of having lessons, problems, and crises in their lives because they see them as the very opportunities that are essential for personal, professional, and spiritual growth. In other words, not only do they expect the difficulties, they need and even welcome them as the ways and means for growth.

They hold to them also, perhaps unawares, because they provide enormous vocational opportunities. Think for a moment of all the vocations that seek to address the learning of lessons and the solving of problems. Everything from teachers to therapists to consultants to managers to psychologists to some rather noted talk show hosts (think Jerry Springer!).

Each has a vested interest in having lessons and problems to address. They serve as their source of income, and as the source of some other rather important things in their life, such as esteem, power, and purpose.

Not only do they have a vested, although perhaps unconscious, interest in lessons and problems, but also in their continuation and proliferation. Again, it's the source of their livelihood and a great deal of the meaning and purpose they find in life, and they've got to keep them coming in order to have those things. The thought of living without them is simply unacceptable to them.

Consider, too, the number of vocations created and sustained by crises—everything from medical doctors and emergency personnel of every stripe, to TV news directors, to public relations experts. And again, they, too, have a vested interest in not only addressing the various crises, but keeping them going. I recently overheard the chief administrator of a local hospital say to her surgical staff, "Go out there and drum up more surgical patients. We need the business!" And this from a rather kind and generous person, who simply needed such things in order to keep the hospital profitable so that it could continue to provide jobs for the doctors, nurses, and staff who worked there. Not to mention her own position!

Note here that I'm not saying that such persons necessarily have a *conscious* intention for lessons, problems, and crises to continue or proliferate. It's simply a part of their worldview and their conscious and unconscious expectations. For them, it's the "way life is." It's their "reality." And since this is the way life is, then the best way to address it is by becoming good managers of its difficulties, and making the most of them.

The second worldview takes a completely different perspective. If the first worldview sees life as difficult, uncer-

47

tain, and filled with fearful circumstances, and deems the addressing of those difficulties—the lessons, problems, and crises—to be necessary for us to find meaning and purpose in our lives and to grow into wholeness, the second type sees life, for the most part, to offer joy and bliss, and to be only as difficult, uncertain, and fearful as we choose to make it.

While in the first worldview, we are left to our own resources to address the fears, the uncertainties, and the difficulties, the second asserts that there is guidance—Divine Guidance—available to us to help us avoid them. And it sees most of the difficulties to be but the consequences of our own actions apart from the Divine Guidance—what often happens when we do not acknowledge and follow the Divine Guidance as it comes to us.

In this second worldview, the fearful difficulties are seen as perhaps inevitable, but *not* as necessary. They are inevitable because even for those who seek to follow the Divine Guidance, there are times when, for whatever reason, they don't, and the consequences inevitably follow. However, the consequences—the fearful difficulties—are not seen as necessary for growth into wholeness. Wholeness can come—perhaps best—by simply following the Divine Guidance.

As you may imagine, the differences in these two worldviews are sizable! Although I won't go into all the differences, I'll give enough here for you to get the idea.

In the first worldview, life is *intended* to be difficult, filled with one fearful circumstance after another. It's the nature of the created order, and we'd better just accept that as fact. It's simply our destiny to have to confront daily the uncertainty and the fearful difficulties of life, and we'd best learn well how to do it.

In the second worldview, life is intended to be happy and blissful, not difficult at all. In this model, each of us has endless possibilities for joy, abundance, and peace, and all that's necessary to realize these possibilities is to follow God's Divine Guidance.

In the first, the difficulties—the lessons, problems, and crises—are not only to be expected, but also seen as necessary for our growth into wholeness. They are seen as the very ways that growth happens for us. In this view, we have two choices, either to do nothing and be victimized by the difficulties, or to learn to handle them by becoming skilled and courageous lesson-learners, problem-solvers, and crises-survivors.

In the second, the difficulties are seen as mostly the result of our own actions. Here, our choices for response are twofold. We can either continue to rely on ourselves—do what we've always done, and get what we've always gotten—which may mean having to deal with the fearful difficulties as we bring them to ourselves through our actions. Or we can change our behavior and avoid the difficulties—at least most of them—altogether! In this view, the difficulties can be used not so much to grow toward wholeness as to produce awareness of how we can "wake up," change our behavior, follow the Divine Guidance, and avoid most of the difficulties in the future.

In the first, as we expect the difficulties, we tend to create them. It's a matter of drawing to us what we expect to draw to us—of seeing what we *think* or *believe* we see.

In the second, we don't tend to draw difficulties to us because we aren't expecting them to come to us. Instead, we draw to us the expected bliss.

49

In the first worldview, because difficulties are seen as a part of the created order, as both necessary and expected, then we *have* to deal with them. Either that, or be victimized by them. We have no other choice.

In the second, because difficulties are not seen as a necessary part of the created order, we can choose to manage our behavior in ways that allow us to follow the Divine Guidance and therefore avoid most of them altogether.

In the first, we are left to our own level of courage, intellect, and resources to handle the various difficulties as they invariably come to us. And depending on how courageous, smart, and resourceful we are, we can either handle them successfully, or be victimized by them. In this model, we are fairly vulnerable, depending on how adept we are at successfully handling the difficulties.

In the second, we are no longer so vulnerable or left to handle the difficulties ourselves. For in this model, we have at our disposal the constancy of Divine Guidance to lead us forth as we negotiate life.

In the first, life *is* difficult! And the best we can do is deal with it and hope for the best.

In the second, life is not difficult at all. It's easy. In fact, life is only as difficult as we make it. We can choose to follow the Divine Guidance and then know life as bliss!

As you can see, the particular worldview that you choose to believe determines, to a large degree, your experience of life. You can choose to see life as uncertain, fearful, and difficult, and so it will be. Or you can choose to see it as bliss, follow the Divine Guidance that is available to you, and bliss it will be!

How you see, and therefore experience, life is a choice. And believe me, it *is* your choice. And the choice you make will determine all the difference in how you experience your life. For life is a matter of perception. Change your perception, and you change your life. So, what will it be?

In our souls everything moves guided by a mysterious
hand.
We know nothing of our own souls that are
ununderstandable and say nothing.

The deepest words of the wise man teach us the same as
the whistle of the wind when it blows or the sound of the
water when it is flowing.

Antonio Machado (1875-1939), *TheEnlightened Heart*

NECESSARY UNDERSTANDINGS

Three Notions of the Nature of Humanity

AT THIS POINT you may be asking, if navigating our life is as easy as following the Divine Guidance that God gives to us, then why is our experience of life often so fearful and difficult? Why don't we just follow the Divine Guidance and live in bliss?

The reasons are fairly simple. The most obvious reason is that most people do not know that Divine Guidance is even available to them. This is why it remains such a secret—most don't know it exists. They still believe that they're pretty much on their own to guide themselves through life. Or if they do experience the guidance, through an inkling, a nudge, or a message, they may call it something else, not believing it really is Divine Guidance, and, therefore, not affording it any credibility.

Or they may believe that perhaps such guidance is available, but do not, for one reason or another, choose to avail themselves of it. Instead they continue to look to themselves or to others for information that they hope will point them in the right direction.

Therefore, because they either do not know about, believe, or avail themselves of Divine Guidance, they invariably suffer the inevitable and difficult consequences of not following such guidance, which include the aforementioned categories of lessons, problems, and crises.

Think for a moment about how you typically go about getting the guidance you need to live your life. If you're like most, you probably spend a great deal of time rationally gathering information through your five senses, discerning what's true and trustworthy, and sorting out the possibilities. You may throw in a measure of worry and anxiety, a few frets, and some self-doubts. Then, with as much certainty as you can muster, and perhaps with a little fear and trembling, you gird yourself with as much courage as you can gather and you make your decisions. And hope for the best!

Then, like most, you may find yourself perplexed when life didn't turn out the way you had hoped, and you are dealing with more difficulties than you'd like. In fact, there may be times when life itself begins to feel really precarious, fearful, and difficult. And you may find yourself again asking why life has to be that way—why having a happy, fulfilling life can't just be easier.

A part of the difficulty lies in the fact that there are at least three notions of the basic nature of humanity and our human condition. And each notion determines to a large degree to whom or to what we look in order to get the information and guidance we need to navigate this journey of life.

One notion is that from birth we are at odds with God. This position, as recorded in the story of Adam and Eve in the Torah and the Bible, says that from the very beginning, humankind has been born in a rebellious and sinful state. As such, in order to escape the condemnation of God, we are to strive to change our ways and live a Godly life, in hopes that God will accept us again, forgive us, and save us from the inevitable consequences of our sinfulness.

Many who believe in this position believe that God doesn't need to speak to us today because God has already spoken in scripture, and that that is where we must go for the guidance we need to live our lives. They take the position that any "guidance" that comes from sources other than or outside scripture is, at best, suspect. Some would go so far as to say that such guidance is either a manifestation of our own human desires or even demonic forces, and should be specifically avoided!

The main problem with this model is that these writings, as primary sources of guidance, especially when taken literally, are often hard to understand, and at times present conflicting information. The stories were set in a time far different from ours, with different attitudes and beliefs. Even accomplished biblical scholars have difficulty coming to agreement on certain critical issues and understandings that impact how one is to live one's life. Even our own history will confirm that the scriptures have been used to substantiate just about anything various persons, usually those in power, have wanted confirmed, from slavery, to the treatment of women, to racism and prejudice in all its forms.

That's not to say that there is not legitimate guidance in scripture, for there surely is. In fact, the scriptures can be one of the valued sources of Divine Guidance. My point is that God is not restricted to only these writings for God's Divine Guidance to us.

And furthermore, it doesn't make logical sense that God would choose to communicate with God's people for a period of time, the time-spans covered in the scriptural accounts, and then have no interest in more current and active communication with them. Surely a God who values relationships would have more interest than that.

Be that as it may, many people still seek to rely solely on the scriptures for their source of guidance. And many of those same people find themselves often confused and frustrated because they can't decipher a clear path for their life.

A second notion of the nature of our humanity is that we are created as separate and separated individuals, and that we exist solely in our individuality. This position maintains that we are to be able to navigate life primarily by gathering information through our five senses, using our rational faculties to sort it all out, and then making our own decisions based on that information.

Under this model, we are primarily, if not solely, responsible for getting the information we need to lead our lives. We are left basically to our own intelligence and ingenuity. We each must fend for ourselves. We must be smart enough and clever enough to get the right information, and then be intelligent enough and courageous enough to make the right decisions to navigate the course safely and without mishap.

Under this model we are vulnerable, at least to the degree of our own intelligence and resources, and life can be fairly fragile. We can experience much anxiety, and fear can rule our minds and hearts. Under this model there are no certainties, unless we make them so. And even then, the certainties are a function of our own abilities, and are still subject to unforeseen happenings. Setting sail on this journey is, at best, a risk. And yet, under this model, by virtue of our birth, we have no choice but to set sail, and hope for the best.

Many, if not most, of us live our lives as if this model were true. We hit the ground running everyday, gathering, sorting, sifting, deciding as best we can. And all the while, we are hoping, praying, keeping our fingers crossed that nothing unforeseen comes along to blind-side us and knock us off course. We pray that the stock market holds its own, that the on-coming driver stays in her lane, that the children are safe, that our spouse won't find somebody else, that our job will be there tomorrow, that our health will remain good, and on and on and on.

On our more conscious days, we realize that our life has become a series of difficulties, an onslaught of lessons and problems and crises, with which we must deal. "That's just life!" we say, as if to somehow give our minds, our hearts, and even our souls some degree of consolation, or at least help us make sense out of the chaos in which we live.

In order to cope with it all and ease the pain and suffering as we attempt to create some measure of certainty, we try as best we can to become excellent lesson-learners, problem-solvers, and crisis-survivors. We even create whole vocations around such things, no doubt as a way to better equip ourselves *to* cope, and also as ways to earn our income, structure our time, keep ourselves on course, give ourselves a sense of purpose, a modicum of importance, a degree of success, and at least some semblance of security. And as we become more and more accustomed to such roles, and even dependent on them for our livelihood, it's just that much harder to want to find ways to give them up.

So, we then convince ourselves that difficulties, the lessons, problems, and crises, are but a natural and even necessary part of life. And we find it all but ludicrous when someone suggests that maybe, just maybe, they are not necessary. We may even find ourselves getting irritated when someone suggests that life is not intended to be like that at all—that there may be a better way to live—one in which we don't have to be vulnerable to and suffer such difficulties at all.

Remember, too, that for many, their vocations are based on keeping the difficulties going. Without lessons to learn, problems to solve, and crises to survive many of us would be out of work—which I guess would be okay, for that at least would give us a problem to solve or maybe even a crisis to survive!

When things get really difficult under this model, when we get tired of learning lessons, solving problems, and trying to survive crises, especially when those things are personal, we find ourselves saying things like "Surely there must be a better way!" And all the while "reality," as well as our economic and social structure, not to mention many theological and philosophical constructs, our parents, our family, our friends, and just about anybody else to whom we care to listen, are all telling us that there is not.

And yet, *my* intent here is to show you that there is!

The answer is to be found in the third model of our human condition as alluded to above. Under this model, we understand ourselves to be precious children of God, whom God loves unconditionally. God, like any loving parent, is constantly seeking to give us, as precious children, the loving guidance we need to live our lives in joy and peace.

This model takes as one of its basic tenets the notion that life's difficulties, including lessons, problems, and crises, are not necessarily inevitable in our lives. Rather, they are often the inevitable *consequences* of not following the direct Divine Guidance (described in Part II of this book) that is constantly made available to us. In other words, the notion is that if we get and use the direct Divine Guidance that God is constantly making available to us, through inklings, nudges, and messages, then we can avoid most of life's difficulties, including lessons, problems, and crises.

This notion of truth set forth in this third model is based on a lifetime of personal study, meditation, struggles, trial and error, and personal experience. It is also based on the personal experience of others gleaned through personal interviews and through their stories that they've kindly shared with me—many of which are included in this book.

From all of this has come the belief that we have been created, not simply as sinful and fallen individuals left to fend for ourselves, but rather as a precious and divine part of an integrated whole under a divine order of creation. As such, we are all connected within that divine order as part of a harmonious whole.

This model further maintains that while we can function as individuals, as in the previous model, we do have another alternative. Rather than simply seeing ourselves solely as individuals, left to rely only on our five senses and our own ingenuity, intelligence, resourcefulness, and rationality to gather, sort, and decide, we have the option of seeing ourselves as part of an integrated whole which has available limitless sources of Divine Guidance.

As part of this integrated whole, we have both the possibility and the opportunity of getting the information and guidance we need directly from the Creator of the Universe, and can thus avoid the otherwise inevitable and difficult consequences of lessons, problems, and crises. Through a constant transmission of information, Divine Guidance is directed to each one of us in our own particular situation and for our own good, and yet in ways which also maintain the harmony, integrity, and common good of the whole.

Our first task under this model is to decide to believe it true, so that we can begin to learn to read and trust the language of Divine Guidance. As we do so, then we can begin to use this Divine Guidance as it comes to us to live happy, productive, and abundant lives, in harmony and peace with all of life.

Effortlessly,
Love flows from God into man,
Like a bird
Who rivers the air
Without moving her wings.
Thus we move in His world
One in body and soul,
Though outwardly separate in form.
As the Source strikes the note,
Humanity sings—
The Holy Spirit is our harpist,
And all strings
Which are touched in Love
Must sound.
—Mechthild of Magdeburg (1210-1297), *The Enlightened Heart*

Necessary Understandings

My Basic Underlying Principle

A S YOU MIGHT have guessed, this book takes as its basic underlying principle that the third notion of the nature of humanity and of the human condition is true. It takes as truth that we are each born as a vital part of a larger created order, and that the Creator of the Universe itself, out of great and gracious love for us, seeks to lead us into a life of joy and abundance as a part of this harmonious whole.

This book also takes as a general observed truth that most of us no longer trust or even know that God seeks to give us such Divine Guidance. Therefore, the book takes as one of its basic tasks the teaching of the skills needed for learning to recognize, read, and trust the language of this Divine Guidance, so that we can then use this Divine Guidance to lead us into being happy and contented human beings who can navigate through life in union, in harmony, and in peace with all of life.

Regardless of which model it is to which you presently subscribe, and just how much relevance you may give to it, I invite you to consider the possibility that the third is the only true model. Consider how your life might be different if you believed it were true, and weren't left to your own devices to get the guidance you need to negotiate your life.

Visualize what life could be like for you if you learned and made us of the skills of recognizing, reading, and following the Divine Guidance of God. Would your life be easier? Would you have fewer fears? Would you feel less precarious and more certain? Would you feel less fragile and more confident? Would you have far more assurance in your life's destiny? Would there be fewer lessons to learn, problems to solve, and crises to handle? Would you be far more productive? Would you have more time and energy to enjoy life, without having to spend so much of it dealing with all the difficulties? Would you have a greater sense of freedom? Would you be happier and more content? And would you enjoy more peace?

My hope is that when you finish reading this book you will be able to answer all the above questions with a resounding "Yes!" And if so, then you can be well on your way to following God's Divine Guidance to the life of joy and abundance that God wills for you!

Therefore, I invite and encourage you to consider the possibilities. Be ready to brace yourself as you become aware that God, out of God's great and gracious love for you, is constantly flooding you with Divine Guidance and its consequent goodness! Be willing to make use of it. Then be ready for a life the likes of which you've only dreamed, full of happiness, fulfillment, abundance, and, perhaps most importantly, peace.

My love and encouragement goes with you. Godspeed!

363-OVER

Come to me, all who labor and are heavy laden, and I will give you rest. Take my yoke upon you, and learn from me; for I am gentle and lowly in heart, and you will find rest for your souls. For my yoke is easy, and my burden is light.

—Jesus, as recorded in Matthew 11: 28-30, *An Inclusive-Language Lectionary, Year A*

PART II

Direct Divine Guidance

God, out of God's great and gracious love for us, is constantly seeking to provide Divine Guidance to us so that we might more easily and peacefully live a life of joy and abundance. In Part II, I will set forth the three kinds of Divine Guidance that God seeks to give to us directly, which include inklings, nudges, and messages.

In the three chapters that follow, I will define, describe, and illustrate each type of Direct Divine Guidance. I will give some clues as to how we lost our natural ability to recognize, acknowledge, trust, and use each particular type, why we often miss the guidance when it comes, and why we must relearn the skill. I will share several real-life stories that further illustrate each type, how each was used or ignored, and the consequences in each instance.

Next, I will invite you to remember occasions in your own life when you have been aware that such guidance was made available to you. I will ask you to reflect on what use, if any, you made of it, and what happened when either you did or did not follow it.

Then, I will provide information to teach you skills that will help you get proficient in recognizing, acknowledging, and making use of each type of guidance. And finally, I will give some insight into what I'm calling a better way—reaching that state of being in which we can make constant use of the myriad attempts of Divine Guidance that God seeks to give to us, so that, indeed, we can live a life of joy and abundance in peace.

It is important to note here that even as you get proficient at making use of the Divine Guidance in whatever forms in which it comes, there *will* be times when it may not *seem* forth-coming. You may find yourself looking, waiting, expecting it, and it's not obvious to you that it is there. Those are precisely the times when you will have to claim the assurance that, indeed, it *is* there, but it may not look like you expected it to look.

For example, once after a move, I was looking for suitable housing. After a rather exhausting search, I found the house I thought I wanted, only to meet one delay after another. I was starting to get really frustrated, and was puzzled as to why God wasn't giving me guidance. Finally, I backed off and just sat with the situation for a while. In the midst of my waiting, a friend told me of another house that was available, one that much better—in fact, perfectly—met my needs and desires. I then realized that God's guidance had been there, at work in my life, all along. My problem, the one I created for myself, and the source of my frustration, was that even though I *thought* I was looking to God's guidance, actually I was trying to get ahead of God and do it on my own. I was grateful for God's timing and for the further confirmation of the constancy of God's Divine Guidance.

I pray that you find the practical method I've set forth in the following chapters helpful and useful. For I believe it can make a significant difference to you personally and to the harmony of our world as each of us learns to recognize, trust, and use God's Divine Guidance. Your happiness, as well as the peaceful co-existence of us all, may well depend on it.

363-OVER

I will instruct you and teach you the way you should go;
I will counsel you with my eye upon you.

Psalm 32:8, *An Inclusive-Language Lectionary, Year B*

DIRECT DIVINE GUIDANCE

The First Attempt: Inklings

WHILE THE GOD of the Universe can use any of the three types of Direct Divine Guidance with us at any given time, perhaps the first type that God may attempt is through what I've called *inklings*. Inklings are those ever-so-subtle signs intended to direct us that can come to us at any time throughout the course of a day. They may come as soft impulses, fleeting thoughts, vague awarenesses, brief insights, intuitive feelings, or inner knowings.

They often come quickly and are gone in the blink of the eye, like seeing the quick wave of a friend about to pass in the oncoming traffic. They appear, as if out of nowhere, and because of their relative mild intrusiveness into our lives, they are often soon gone without much fanfare. Then, as if nothing of importance had happened, we can be well on our way down the road of life without much thought of them, or perhaps even without noticing them at all.

Because of their relative speed, softness, and low impact, they are easy to miss, and perhaps even easier to dismiss. And if we don't know of their existence, or if we are out of practice in acknowledging and heeding such signs, they can escape our awareness altogether! Add to this the frenetic pace of much of our lives, as well as all the ways that we are bombarded with noise, stress, and information that has little to do with us, not to mention the loud rumble of congested thoughts flying around in our heads, and it's easy to see why we often don't notice or heed these subtle inklings.

Because most people simply assume that they're on their own to dig up and sort out the information and the guidance they need to live their lives, they're not expecting or looking for *any* sort of Divine Guidance, much less something so subtle as an inkling. Therefore, they can miss them very easily.

And even if they were made aware of the availability of Divine Guidance, they would probably be very skeptical. For again, the emphasis for most is on self-reliance, looking to their own intelligence, experience, and resourcefulness, or to those about them, to get what they need to live their life. The thought of Divine Guidance, even if it enters their mind, is quickly dismissed as perhaps, at best, some sort of New Age nonsense.

This easy dismissal is especially true of guidance that comes in such a non-invasive and subtle form as does an inkling. Most of us tend to wait for something bold and dramatic, like lightning bolts, earthquakes, or meteor showers. Not something as soft and light as an inkling!

Therefore, sometimes it's only in hindsight that we can be mindful of the attempts of God through inklings to get our attention and give us the guidance we need to live our lives. And sometimes the consequences of dismissing them can be rather serious.

In my work as a marriage and family therapist, I've talked with numerous couples of which either one or both of the parties had inklings, fleeting thoughts in the midst of their wedding, that they should not proceed with the marriage. Unfortunately, all dismissed the inklings rather quickly, and wound up in painful marriages which often ended in divorce.

The reasons they dismissed such subtle signs are rather obvious. They range from embarrassment at the thought of stopping the service, to notions of normality at feeling afraid on such an important occasion, to a sense of duty to follow through on a previous commitment. They include the thought of what others, including the other party, family, and invited guests, would think if they stopped the service, to the realization that they had paid a great deal of money to do this and couldn't justify calling it off at this point.

On a personal note, the same thing happened with me. I had an inkling in the midst of getting dressed for the wedding ceremony that I shouldn't be getting married. I dismissed it as just nervous jitters. I got another inkling as I stood there before the congregation as my fiancé began her walk down the aisle. I even remember saying to myself as she drew nearer to the chancel area, "You have to put a smile on your face so the guests and family members out there will think you're happy." But by that time, of course, it seemed too late to stop the ceremony. And besides, again I dismissed it as but a further sign of nervousness. In hindsight, perhaps I should have heeded the inklings, for after years of struggle, coun-

seling, and much pain and suffering, I accepted the consequences of failing to heed the inklings, and filed for divorce.

In light of the rather serious and painful consequences in
these particular examples, the reasons for dismissal of the
inklings seem rather lame, at least in 20-20 hindsight! However, at the time I'm sure that they all seemed more than
reasonable. It wasn't until later that we realized the importance, and truth, of our inklings—as well as the consequences
of not heeding them!

When the inklings *are* heeded, however, the consequences
can be vastly different. I have a friend, Julia, who has a rather
keen and developed sense of her inklings. She makes use of
them all the time, in everything from when and where to go
shopping to get the best deals, to with whom she needs to
make contact, to what she needs to do each day that will
prove to be the most productive. She's told stories of having
an inkling in the form of a rather subtle sense that she needed
to call someone with whom she hadn't had contact in awhile.
Acting on her inkling, she would discover that she had called
at an important time, and was very glad she had followed
through.

For example, once Julia had an inkling to call her old
college roommate with whom she hadn't talked in a number
of years. Heeding the soft impulse, she dialed the number.
Her friend answered, in tears. She had just been diagnosed
with breast cancer, was alone, and was in desperate need of a
friend with whom to talk.

Julia tells me that this happens time and again in her life.
In fact, it happens so often, that she has learned to pay keen
attention, to heed and act on these inklings. And she notes
that her life has been far richer for it.

My friend, Sandy, tells this story of an inkling. After marrying her husband in July of 1994, she had not made a trip without him in over four years. They had always enjoyed traveling together, and it was unusual for them to be apart. However, in September of 1998, in the midst of her husband's busiest season at work, she had an inkling to take a long weekend off and fly to Atlanta with her daughter to see her Mom and Dad. They all had a delightful visit, made some nice photos, and had several good talks. She had no way of knowing that it would be the last time she would see her Dad alive. He died less than one month later. Sandy said she considers it a great kindness and a source of deep comfort that God would encourage her and her daughter to visit and share that time with her Dad, since they normally only saw each other once or twice a year.

An acquaintance of mine, Ted, shared a story with me recently regarding his experience with inklings. He was on a wilderness camping trip alone. He had hiked about fifteen miles into the back country, and had enjoyed several nights camping by himself. When supplies ran low, he decided to make his way out of the woods and head for home. As he began his way out, he discovered that his compass was not working. To make things even more difficult, the sky had heavy cloud cover, which further limited his sense of direction. He decided to sit for a moment to gather his thoughts before he proceeded any further. Feeling more composed, he began again, this time with a vague sense of direction. As he put it, he just "followed his nose" and was led back to the trail that would lead him home.

As I pressed Ted on his experience, I asked him if this was not just some coincidence, or perhaps some innate ability of his. Ted was convinced that he had experienced a form of Divine Guidance. He was sure that he was being led out

·

75

of the woods by a Power greater than his own abilities, and that what he had experienced was not just chance or luck. Ted was convinced that he had had an inkling, a subtle, but certain, bit of Divine Guidance, and that, for whatever reason, he had chosen to follow it to his safety.

Anita relayed a story of an inkling obeyed. She was leaving her house one morning, in a hurry to get to work. She had much to do that day, and she didn't want to be late. She was already feeling hassled, trying to get her children off to school, getting the pets fed, and then having her meditation time interrupted by a phone call. As she was scurrying out the door, she had an inkling that she should stop to gather her thoughts. As she did, she got a second inkling that she should go check to see if she had extinguished the candle she had used in her meditation. She discovered that in her haste to answer the phone, she had forgotten to blow out the candle. Because she trusted her inklings, she avoided what would have surely been a tragedy.

Sam related a story of an inkling ignored, and the resulting consequences. He had had his new car serviced at the local dealership before leaving for vacation. They were supposed to change the oil as a part of the service. He had packed the car prior to going to the dealership, so he could be on his way directly from there when they had finished servicing it. When he went to pick it up, he had an inkling to check the oil himself before driving it, to make sure they had replaced the oil when they had drained out the old. Thinking such an oversight to be silly, he ignored the inkling. Thirty miles outside of town, on a lonely stretch of road, his car began making a horrible noise. He checked the oil—the dipstick was dry as a bone, and the engine was burned up! And his vacation plans were greatly affected.

Steven told of an inkling ignored that altered his life. Steven has adult-on-set diabetes, and must monitor his blood regularly to avoid toxic shock from an imbalance in his blood sugar. On one particular day, he began to feel low energy. Thinking that his insulin was out of balance, he checked his blood several times. Each time, the reading came back okay. While he did have an inkling that the new meter he had just purchased may have been calibrated wrong, he dismissed it. Rather, he thought that he must just be getting a cold, which would account for the way he was feeling, and so he didn't worry much about it. The next morning he awoke in a hospital room, with his wife standing next to his bed. She had found him collapsed on the floor when she arrived home from work the evening before, the result of toxic shock. The meter had indeed been wrongly calibrated, and if she had not found Steven when she did, he probably would have died. Steven concluded that he would now pay much more attention to his inklings!

Sometimes following one's inklings makes our lives much simpler. Jerome, who is in the water-systems business, and who has to coordinate his work with other contractors such as electricians, told me this story. He was heading toward an out-of-town job and was thinking about a second upcoming job. This second job was going to be difficult because of snow and mud, and he wanted to finish it before even worse conditions prevailed. He wanted to contact the electrician to inform him of what materials he would need to complete the job and to give him sufficient time to get those materials, but his office had no way to contact him. As Jerome was driving through town, he had an inkling to follow a route he usually did not take. As he took the new route, the electrician with whom he needed to talk was getting something out of his truck, saw Jerome approaching, hailed him down, and they discussed the new job.

Sometimes inklings can lead to even more miraculous experiences of God's presence and care in our lives. My dear friend, Ginger, related this story. Her father and stepmother were on vacation in Mexico City, and as her father got out of the cab and started to pay the fare, he had a massive heart attack and died instantly. Her stepmother, Ruth, knew no one in Mexico City, did not speak Spanish, and was unaware that every death in Mexico had to be investigated by the police.

In her despair and grief, Ruth, a very sensible, logical woman, began considering what to do next. Suddenly, a young man appeared, said his name was Michael and was from the conciliate, and offered help. Normally Ruth would have refused assistance from a total stranger, especially in a strange and foreign place, choosing instead to rely on her own abilities and resources. However, as he approached, Ruth had this inner knowing, an inkling, that he could be trusted. With her consent, Michael knelt down next to her husband, said a prayer, and then proceeded to help her take care of everything, even offering her money if she needed it. As he took her back to her hotel, he handed her a card with his phone number hand-written on the back.

Later, Ruth tried to reach the young man to thank him for all his assistance and kindness, but got no answer at the number he had given her. She then tried to reach him at the conciliate, but they said they knew of no one there named Michael.

Ruth is convinced that because she was willing to heed the inkling, God was able to send another miracle—an angel named Michael to assist her. She realized that that encounter not only relieved her of enormous responsibilities, but also helped ease her grief at the loss of her husband. She was grateful for such tangible signs of God's love and care for her!

Perhaps you've had similar experiences. A thought flashes through your mind. You have an intuitive feeling. You experience an inner knowing. You have a quick impulse to take some action. Perhaps you're prompted to call someone, or check something out, or say something. You feel a subtle prompting to do something that you wouldn't otherwise know to do.

Then what happens? Do you heed the inkling and take the action? Do you make the call? Do you check the thing out? Do you say what you've been prompted to say? Or do you dismiss it, only to discover later reasons why you wished you had followed your inkling?

And if you did dismiss it, why did you dismiss it so easily? Did you dismiss it as but another fleeting thought among the millions that pass through your mind everyday? Or did you perhaps let your "rational" mind take over, and convince you that the inkling was but a silly fear or an absurd, even mindless, thought? What were the reasons? Did it seem foolish, embarrassing, or unimportant? And what were the resulting consequences?

Have you ever trusted an inkling? Have you ever had evidence that heeding inklings is important? What difference did heeding them make in your life? Were the consequences different than if you had not heeded them? Significantly so?

I encourage you to identify and consider the inklings that have come to you. Remember how you handled them, and why you did what you did. What have been the consequences

---

79

of your actions? How would you handle differently the situations in which you have ignored the inkling if you could do it over again? Or would you?

And how do you know when that fleeting thought, that vague awareness, that brief insight, or that inner knowing is really an inkling, and not just one of a million thoughts that clutter your mind. How do you know it's not just fear in disguise? How do you know when to trust it, and when to ignore it? How do you know, especially in the rush of the moment, whether to act on the impulse or dismiss it as unimportant?

These are all very important questions for us to consider, especially if we are to be adept at taking our inklings seriously. To adequately address these concerns, at least four things are needed: an attitude of trust, a sense of expectancy, the skill of discernment, and the discipline of practice.

The first thing we have to do in order to make use of our inklings is to develop an attitude of trust. We must trust that the God of the Universe does indeed love us, wants what's best for us, and is willing to give us the guidance we need in order to help us get it. We must trust that God is able to send us inklings, and that such inklings are trustworthy, and are intended for our good. And we must trust that these inklings are one of God's ways of giving us the guidance we need to live life in joy and abundance.

Without such trust and assurance in the benevolence of the God of the Universe to give us the guidance we need, we won't trust the inklings we receive. We will have little or no reason to trust them. In fact, we probably won't even notice them! And if we should notice them, we probably won't acknowledge them, or give them any credibility. Instead, we'll dismiss them as quickly as they came.

As we dismiss the inklings, we will then, of course, suffer whatever consequences which may follow, thinking perhaps that's it's just been a bit of bad luck. We won't realize that we had the opportunity, even the responsibility to ourselves and our own well-being, as well as to others and to that which has been entrusted to us, to notice the inklings, acknowledge them, and follow their lead!

Ignoring or dismissing inklings is more than just a matter of ignorance or negligence. It is, in fact, a matter of being irresponsible, and but another way that we may fail to take care of ourselves, our minds, bodies, spirits, and relationships. It's also irresponsible with regard to how well we fulfill our duties as good stewards of all that is entrusted to us. And as noted above, the consequences can be not only destructive and even deadly for ourselves, but perhaps for the whole world!

So, as you can see, trusting in the goodness and benevolence of the God of the Universe and God's willingness to send us inklings is of prime importance. It serves as the basis of our getting the Divine Guidance we need, and of insuring harmony in all the created order.

Once we've established that God is trustworthy and is willing to send us inklings, the second thing we must learn is to develop a sense of expectancy. We must begin to expect that inklings will come to us, and come often! We must take on the attitude that as ones loved by the God of the Universe, it's not only our privilege, but also our divine right to get such guidance, and to trust that the guiding inklings will come as often as we need them. We must begin to realize and accept as fact that Divine Guidance is our birthright as precious children of God.

<hr />

81

As we develop an attitude of expectation, we will come to expect the inklings in all the various situations that we find ourselves, even when we may not be aware that we need such guidance. Expecting the inklings will become second nature to us, much like a child who knows she is loved by her parents expects her parents to carefully and lovingly look out for her. She expects them to gently guide her in the ways she should go, all without her asking, knowing to ask, or even knowing for what to ask. She is free to live her life to the fullest, in all its wonder and beauty, because she is confident that her parents will be there for her, gently and lovingly giving her the guidance she needs, precisely when she needs it, and in the ways that will insure her happiness.

The third thing we must do if we are to be adept at following our inklings is to learn the skill of discernment. We must be able to discern which thoughts are inklings and which are not, so that we can be assured that we are following God's Divine Guidance and not some errant thought of our own.

Although discernment was a natural ability for us as children, most of us will discover that we have to relearn it as adults. The reasons are two-fold. First, many of us have been carefully trained out of that skill by some of those same people who so lovingly took care of us when we were very small children. As parents or primary caretakers, they saw it to be *their* duty to provide the guidance we needed, and therefore we weren't enabled or allowed to cultivate our natural ability to get the guidance directly from the God of the Universe. Rather we were taught and expected to depend on them to be our source of guidance.

As we continued to grow and mature, as part of their notion of continued care for us, they began to teach *us* ways to gather the information we needed to make our own decisions. They began to transfer the responsibility from themselves to us. This was considered good parenting, as well as good training, in order for us to become self-sufficient. The more skills we were taught to become self-sufficient, the less we remembered about how to rely on God for Divine Guidance. We simply looked to ourselves and our own ingenuity, and we lost all remnants of our natural ability. Thus, now we have to relearn it!

The second reason we have to learn again this skill is due to the fact that in our information society, we are bombarded on every side with information and thoughts. Our minds process millions of bits of information in the course of a day. We have thousands of thoughts racing through our minds, and many of us are juggling several tasks at once. Because our reliance has been on our own self-sufficiency to gather information and then make decisions based on that information rather than on relying on God for Divine Guidance, we find ourselves on information-overload, and we no longer trust our ability to discern what's divine and what's not. We must learn again some reliable way to make distinctions and discern among all those thoughts as to which are inklings and which are not.

So, how do we learn to discern Divine Guidance, especially something as subtle as an inkling, from all the extraneous thoughts that pop into our mind? Perhaps one of the best ways is to test the source of a thought's motivation. If the source is fear in any form, it probably is not an inkling.

On the other hand, if it has love for us as its motivator, then it may well be an inkling. For remember, the premise here is that the God of the Universe is for us and not against us. God created us in God's own image, loves us, and seeks

———

83

our good. God's motivation in sending us inklings is God's love for us as God seeks to give us the Divine Guidance we need to live a life of happiness and prosperity.

Therefore, the guidance God gives to us would have only love as its motivating factor. God would never seek to fill us with paralyzing fear! For fear would simply defeat God's purpose in giving us Divine Guidance—a free and abundant life.

Therefore, to discern whether you can trust and should act on what appears to be an inkling, ask the question, "Is this subtle awareness, this soft impulse, this ever-so-subtle sign, motivated by love or by fear?" If it's fear, then you can pay no attention to it—let it pass—it's probably not an inkling. If it's love, it probably is an inkling, and can be followed with trust and assurance.

Another reliable way to discern a true inkling of God is to determine if its guidance has as its goal our highest good and the good of all concerned. A true inkling of God will always result in the promotion of the highest good for all who will be affected by its guidance. It will never enable one person or group to have advantage over the other, or for one to succeed at the expense of the other. It will seek the best and highest good for all.

Still another way to discern a true inkling of God is to determine if it will ultimately establish and enable peace, both personally and communally. Although sometimes it may appear to initiate a sense of immediate chaos, perhaps even pain and discomfort, the defining moment is when you can see that finally it will bring about peace. If so, then it is most likely a true inkling of God.

As you acknowledge and work with inklings, or with any

of the forms of God's Divine Guidance, you will get more and more proficient in your discernment. Like anything new, it will take practice—and the practice will be well worth the effort!

The fourth thing we have to do in order to follow our inklings is to develop a discipline of practice. By that, I mean a routine, a habit of following the inklings until it becomes second nature. Such a discipline is required, because most of us have a long history of not heeding our inklings, and of suffering the consequences! Instead of routinely following our inklings, we have tended to yield to both our so-called rationality as well as our self-sufficiency.

Our "rationality" would have us believe that inklings are silly, unreasonable, foolish, embarrassing, or unnecessary. Our "self-sufficiency" would have us rely solely on our own abilities. In order to overcome these resistances, we have to establish a regular discipline of practice—a pattern of almost automatic response—so that we can respond quickly without our usual over-analysis. Without such a discipline, we may well fall victim to our old ways and easily dismiss our inklings, which is fairly understandable and normal in our society because ignoring or dismissing inklings is generally the rule rather than the exception.

If we heed the first three points above, that is, trust the God of the Universe, expect God to provide us with the good guidance we need, and hone our skills of discernment, then developing a discipline of practice will be much easier. We will feel and experience a diminishing sense of resistance, and an increase in positive response, as our skills of trust, expectancy, and discernment increase.

The more we practice, and the more benefit we experience as we make use of our inklings, the stronger our discipline will become, until perhaps one day it will be second nature to us, as it is with my friend, Julia, mentioned above. And what freedom, assurance, and joy we will know as we confidently follow our inklings!

At this point, my encouragement to you is this: Pay attention to your inklings. Acknowledge them. Begin to trust them as best you can. Act on them, even when you aren't quite sure you should. And then pay attention to what happens when you do.

This might all feel somewhat foolish to you at first, even scary. You may feel insecure, timid, and self-conscious. You may not want to tell anybody about it as you begin, which, at this point, may be wise, because the last thing you need now is to be discouraged by their possible unbelief. Let yourself accumulate a history of making use of your inklings as a way to build your own confidence in them before you tell your friends.

Continue to use the inklings as they come to you until it becomes quite natural to you. Acknowledge how much easier and more fulfilling your life has become as a result of the Divine Guidance. And give thanks, acknowledging gratitude to the Spirit who is leading you forth to a life of joy, abundance, and peace.

Then, you're ready to shout it from the rooftops. Tell all who will hear how free and easy—how prosperous and abundant—your life has become because of your reliance on God's Divine Guidance. For the people of the world need to hear of your experience—your testimony—so that they, too, can know the joy and peace of life lived in the Spirit of Divine Guidance!

God is thirsty for everyone.

This thirst has already drawn the Holy to Joy
and we the living are ever being drawn and
drunk.

And yet
God still thirsts and longs.
—Julian of Norwich, *Meditations With Julian of
Norwich*

DIRECT DIVINE GUIDANCE

The Second Attempt: Nudges

THE SECOND TYPE of Direct Divine Guidance that the Spirit may use with you is through what I've called *nudges*. Nudges are similar to inklings, only they aren't quite as subtle. They usually come with a little more force, tend to linger longer, and are usually more persistent.

They come as gentle, but firm, mental pushes, like a friend seeking your attention with the touch of his hand, or by the bumping of her elbow on your arm. They're like focused intuitive hints, much like those given by a loved one to help us solve a puzzle or win a prize. They're like intermittent and persistent thoughts that come into our consciousness with some degree of regularity and intentionality.

Because nudges tend to carry more intensity, they're

somewhat easier to detect than are inklings. And because they tend to persist longer, we have a better chance of actually responding and yielding to their lead.

And yet, as noted with inklings, nudges are every bit as easy to miss and dismiss because, for the most part, we don't teach or emphasize their existence, nor do we train people in how to detect and use them. Thus, because of our relative, or even complete, inexperience in acknowledging, trusting, and acting on them, we can overlook them just as easily as we can inklings.

Add to that the fact that many would find relying on something as intangible as a nudge for a source of guidance, especially when something important is at stake, all but nonsensical and irresponsible, and it's no wonder that nudges don't get much notice.

As with inklings, it may be only after the fact, in hindsight, that we realize we've been nudged! And by then we've probably missed the opportunity for the guidance it afforded us.

To my chagrin, I've had, and unfortunately ignored, lots of nudges—nudges that I now realize, if I had acted on them, would have made me a very wealthy man. For instance, when my children were little, we still used cloth diapers that had to be fastened with rather sharp pins. If you've ever changed a strong, healthy, wriggling twelve-month-old child using cloth diapers and sharp-pointed safety pins, you know how dangerous it can be. Always careful not to stick my child, I would invariably stick myself in the thumb. So much for the so-called "safety" pins!

One day as I was changing my daughter, trying as best I

could to protect her and escape unscathed myself, I had the nudge to create a diaper that fastened without pins. I had that nudge several more times over the next three years of having infant children, especially on those times when I'd prick my thumb again. But I never acted on it. Finally, somebody else did. And now the rest is history. And I'm left to "pamper" my embarrassed and bruised ego—and to regret my meager bank account!

I've also had nudges to invest in certain companies. I didn't, of course, only to watch their stock price continue to rise. The last was a new telecommunications company, which began with something like an eleven dollar offering, which quickly went to eighty dollars, then split two for one. And it continues to do very well.

In my work as a personal and business coach, I hear numerous stories of others who have nudges. Some act on them and some don't. And sometimes, as their coach, I find that it is my job to encourage their response.

Jeff did act on his nudge, and now his life is entirely different. Jeff had grown up in the business community. His father owned a rather large and prosperous firm, and when Jeff graduated from college, his father offered him a position in the firm. Because of his talent, Jeff did quite well for himself. He even branched out on his own also, and started several other companies. He married his childhood sweetheart, had three bright and beautiful children, and continued to prosper.

And yet, despite his success, Jeff wasn't content, at least not like he wanted to be. For he had had this desire for years to try his hand at writing. Yet, making a living at writing didn't

91

seem practical. Nor did he know what kind of writing he wanted to pursue.

Then one day, while watching a travelogue, Jeff had a nudge to be a travel writer. Knowing that others would think him insane to make such a "foolish" move, he sat on the idea. But he didn't dismiss it. And the nudges persisted. He would find himself in the travel section of bookstores, feeling this strong and confident sense that he could write those books. Or he would find himself reading the travel page in the paper, and feeling an insatiable desire to write the editor to inquire as to how he could get started writing articles.

As we began our coaching relationship, knowing of his business career, and feeling a nudge of my own, I asked him what he would do or be if he could do or be anything—if there were no limits. As quick as a wink he said, "I'd be a travel writer!" I then invited and challenged him to pursue it.

Jeff accepted the challenge and eventually shared the idea with his wife. Expecting her to be cool to what seemed like a radical notion, she surprised him—she loved it. She encouraged him in his pursuits—even to the point of arranging to load up the kids and head out for a year to travel the country so he could give it a try.

He then had to share his decision to pursue a new career with his father, with whom he was still in business, and who, nearing retirement age, was assuming Jeff would continue on with the business interests. Expecting his father to be gravely disappointed, Jeff was reluctant to tell him. Mustering up his courage, he finally told his father of his plans. His father's response all but shocked him. He thought it was a grand idea, and shared with Jeff how he wished he had pursued an adventure in his younger years.

Jeff, trusting his nudges, sold his businesses, said farewell to his family and friends, closed up his house, loaded up his family, and headed out. He's now on his way to becoming a successful, happy, and contented writer. In fact, he just won a national award for his work. What a difference a nudge can make!

My father, on the other hand, didn't heed his nudge. Living on a small farm and working for the railroad, he had the nudge to buy up more land and go into farming full-time. The land was affordable, and because he had happy memories of growing up on a farm, he dearly loved it. The railroad, for which he had worked since he was twenty-one, was drudgery for him. It was just a job—a way to make money to support himself and his family. Having lived through the depression though, he was scared to follow his nudge. He stayed on at the railroad for forty-four years, and then died not quite three years after retirement, suddenly, of a heart attack, before he ever fully realized his dream.

I think of my Dad sometimes, with sadness, and wonder how his life, and perhaps mine, would have been different if he had turned loose of his fears and followed his nudge. I am sure he would have had much more joy and satisfaction in his life if he had pursued his dream. And, he might have even lived a longer life, and I would have had much longer to share it with him.

Emily had the nudge to start her own business. Though she had been trained as an accountant, and had a fairly lucrative practice, what she really wanted to do was open a little shop, sell sewing goods, and offer various classes in sewing and quilting. Of course, all her family and friends thought she was crazy for wanting to give up such an important, lucrative, and stable career.

However, one morning as she was preparing for tax season, Emily had a strong nudge to follow her dreams. The next day she resigned, withdrew her savings, and within three months she opened up her shop. She's never been happier.

My friend, Sandy, tells this story. When she was still single and a youth minister at a church near Dallas, Texas, the kids with whom she worked came in one day saying, "We found where you can meet your future husband! It's a religious chat area where you post your message and others reply." When Sandy first considered the notion, it was with great hesitation, because she did not want to start relationships with those she feared might be "wacky, religious zealots." However, as she considered it, she had a strong impulse, a nudge, to go ahead and try it, and to write exactly what she wanted, nothing more and nothing less. She wrote up a message that she thought would surely run off any superficial men. It read: "Delta Burke looks, Roseanne Barr humor seeks John Goodman's body with Michael Landon's heart . . . must be 6' or taller, 40 to 45, live in Dallas, and willing to start a family at 40." She had only one response and his memo was dear and humble. "My dad said if you ever find a stranger without a smile, give him one of yours." A week later they met and, as she put it, it was "love at first weekend."

However, their meeting was not without its anxious moments, requiring yet another nudge to make it happen! The night they were to meet, he was to call when he arrived in Dallas from his home in Lubbock, which should have been between 5:00 and 6:00 P.M. By 9:00, he hadn't called. Sandy was beginning to feel stupid, and stood up! She thought about calling him to see what had happened, but she had a rule—

never call a person who has stood you up! So she got busy doing something else. About an hour later, all at once, she felt compelled to call his house in Lubbock. To her surprise, his mother was waiting by the phone just in case she called, to relate to her that Rodney had forgotten to take her phone number with him. His mother relayed Sandy's phone number and he called her right away. They did go out that night, and fell in love. In relating her story to me, Sandy said, "Thank Goodness I followed the nudge, for he's the love of my life!"

Five years ago I experienced a significant nudge as I was returning home to Texas from a quick trip to my birthplace in Tennessee. About halfway home, I had a strong nudge to move to Colorado. Although I had had the nudges before, I'd always found some excuse. The next day, as I considered the nudge, I called some folks whom I had met on vacation in Colorado the previous year. They had moved to Silverton two years before and had refurbished an old hotel there. I asked them how they liked living in Colorado, and they said they loved it. Two days later I resigned from my job, and prepared to make the move.

Now, having lived here these last five years, it's hard for me to imagine why I didn't respond sooner to the previous nudges, because I never did like living in the Texas heat. I knew I had made the right decision the first summer after my move when the temperatures in Dallas soared to well over a hundred degrees for nearly two straight months, while I had my windows open every night, sleeping under my comforter!

A close friend related her experience with nudges. She had been fighting a severe case of lingering depression. Hers was not simply the bad mood kind, but rather a dark sense of failure on every side. She had no energy to pull herself out of it, and her house reflected her state with scattered clothes and general clutter everywhere. Then in the midst of her depression, she awoke one Saturday morning in May, feeling a strong urge, a nudge, to get out of town for the day. Although this was not typical behavior, especially in her condition, she jumped out of bed, got dressed, bought a round trip ticket to San Antonio, rented a car, and drove to Seaworld. Acknowledging that it was an uncommon, and perhaps impractical, thing to do, something inside her—the nudge—caused her to conclude that it was precisely the right thing for her to do on that particular day.

She walked around Seaworld alone, feeling lackadaisical, enjoying how loved the animals were. Then she made her way over to where visitors are allowed to feed the dolphins. As she began to feed them, she said it was uncanny how this one particular dolphin was teasing her. He'd swim up to her, and fall back into the water and swim another lap. Then, he'd thrust himself up on the step directly in front of her, and let her rub and feed him. She stayed there interacting with this dolphin for hours, amazed at their love and playfulness. Then, suddenly, the thought occurred to her, "my sadness is gone!" She concluded that the dolphin, in his playful interaction with her, had sensed her sadness, and had taken it away.

As she returned home, she realized her depression was completely gone. She felt healed and lifted and extremely grateful. And in the seven years since, her depression has never returned.

Following one's nudges can sometimes be the difference between life and death. Jerome, who owns a pump company and works with water systems, told me this story. The particular system on which he was working consisted of a circuit breaker, disconnect, pressure switch, and the pump. He noticed that the disconnect was in line prior to the pressure switch, which meant that when he shut off the disconnect he was free to work on the pressure switch without fear of electrical shock. As he removed the cover on the pressure switch and was about to loosen the screw to remove the wire, he had a strong nudge to check to make sure the wire didn't have current flowing through it. Thinking that he was sure it didn't, he started again to remove the screw as a second, even stronger, nudge came to him. Deciding to heed the nudge, he checked the wire with his voltage meter. To his surprise, the wire did have current flowing through it, because the disconnect that he had previously shut off had been bypassed internally. Therefore the pressure switch was "live," which meant Jerome might *not* have been if he had not heeded his nudges!

Terri's story is similar. Her life was in turmoil. Her marriage had just ended in divorce, and she was trying as best she could to keep things together. Fighting the onslaught of traffic on Central Expressway in downtown Dallas going to and from work only contributed to her sense of insecurity. One particular morning as she entered the on-ramp, she had a strong sense of dread and fear, as if something terrible was about to happen to her. In the midst of almost paralyzing feelings, she had an inner nudge to be especially careful as she made her way to work. Three miles later, the back wheel of a huge truck suddenly came off and slammed into the passenger side of her car.

Terri is convinced that if she had not heeded the nudge to be extremely alert and careful, she would have surely been injured and perhaps even killed. That event made her keenly aware of God's presence in her life and of God's care for her. She said she felt blessed knowing that God was with her, and confident that she would make it through the other difficulties in her life, too, and be fine.

97

Although following nudges can often be critical to our well being, even to the point of making the difference between life and death, the reasons why we so often fail to recognize, trust, and follow our nudges are not unlike those we give for not following our inklings. We haven't been encouraged, nor trained to follow them. They can seem foolish to us, as well as to those who love and care for us. They're unreasonable, often subtle, intangible, and intuitive. They aren't based on hard evidence, and can't be substantiated with hard facts. We can't offer proof that we will be better off if we follow them.

As with inklings, we must exercise a certain degree of courage to follow our nudges. Not only can they hook our own doubts, they can arouse the doubts of others in our life, too, especially if they have some strong, more "practical" reason to believe that we shouldn't follow them.

Karen had the recurring nudge to be an artist. She had never had formal training, but she always loved to sketch. In fact, in grammar school she was often reprimanded by her teaches because she was sketching rather than paying attention to the subject at hand. When, as a teenager, she shared her nudge with her parents, they laughed at her, saying that was a foolish idea. They would chide her with questions like "How could you ever expect to make a living being an artist?"

Believing that her parents loved her and wanted only the best for her, Karen found it hard to defend herself. So, for the next twenty years Karen resisted her persistent nudges. Instead, she went to college, majored in business, and began a career in public relations. She figured that at least in this arena she would be able to work with other artists and creative people. However, over the years, her nudge persisted.

Finally, on her thirty-fifth birthday, Karen gathered up the courage to take action. She secured a private art instructor, and began to study painting. A year later, she quit her job, and began painting full-time. Her first showing was a huge success. Her parents, who previously harbored doubts, now marvel at her talent—and have felt regret about their previous counsel.

The nudge that Marge had would affect her spiritually, offering concrete evidence that God was, indeed, at work in her life. It would also, literally, contribute to bringing life to others.

Driving toward a luncheon engagement with her husband and a close friend, Marge had a rather strong feeling, a nudge, that she should go and donate blood at the local blood bank after lunch. Though she thought this was a rather unusual notion, she didn't question it. As she enjoyed her lunch, and felt blessed to be with two such dear people in her life, the question came up as to what they would do after lunch. With certainty, Marge said that she was going to donate blood. As they looked at her with bewilderment, she also felt a bit surprised at what she had just verbalized. And yet, she also had a strong sense of the importance of the nudge she had received, and knew she must follow it.

She arrived at the blood bank around 3:00 P.M., and was one of only a few donors there. After making her donation, she ran some errands, bought groceries, and then went home.

As she was unloading her groceries, she heard the news that a commercial passenger jet had crashed at Dallas/Ft.

Worth Airport, and they were in dire need of blood. The news confirmed the reason for her nudge.

She reported to me later that she couldn't articulate the feeling of certainty and trust that she had felt upon receiving the initial nudge earlier that day to go and give blood. And she's thankful that she heeded it, for she said she knew she would have felt remorse if she had not. Her experience renewed and increased her sense of God's continuing presence in her life, and made her feel grateful.

Sometimes the courage to follow one's nudge goes up against standard operating procedures and policies. And yet, to have the courage to follow the nudge can make all the difference between life and death. My friend, Axel, tells this story.

It was 1978, and Axel was a Traffic Officer in Santa Ana, California, with the California Highway Patrol. While on routine patrol, he encountered an auto accident in which the driver had crashed his car into a concrete over-crossing support. As Axel approached the car, several onlookers told him that the driver was already dead.

Axel inspected the car and found the driver slumped over, covered with blood, with his head tilted back. He clearly appeared to be dead. Standard procedure was to leave the body as he found it and call for an ambulance. And yet, Axel had a strong nudge to "do something."

Disregarding standard operating procedure, and even ignoring his own health risks, Axel followed his nudge. He bent over the blood-soaked driver and started mouth-to-mouth resuscitation. After about four minutes, Axel began to feel faint, and asked onlookers for help. They refused, so Axel continued. Within a few more minutes, the driver coughed and revived.

Later Axel learned that the man had been distraught and had actually been trying to commit suicide by wrecking his car. When the man recovered, he was most grateful, and for several years afterward, Axel received Christmas cards from him thanking Axel for saving his life.

Sometimes, however, the courage to follow one's nudges is lacking. And the nudges go unanswered. Arthur tells this story.

From the time he was a small child, Arthur had loved to act. He kept family and friends in awe at his talent. In high school, he starred in all the plays, receiving great reviews. His drama teacher began to point him toward the best acting schools, and offered to help him get a scholarship.

And yet, his family, out of their own concern for his welfare, thoroughly discouraged him from pursuing acting as a career. Instead, they wanted him to be an attorney like his father and grandfather before him. Thinking they knew best, Arthur followed suit. He worked hard at it, built up a solid clientele, and made a prosperous financial income for the next thirty-eight years of his life.

But the sad and unfortunate part of his story is that he never really enjoyed his work, because he never claimed himself—he never claimed his heart's desire. And he never acted again, except, of course, as an attorney!

Paying attention to our nudges, as evidenced by Arthur's story, can mean the difference between fully claiming our own life, following our heart's desire, and merely doing what we think we *should* do to either satisfy others or make the money necessary to pay our bills. It can make the difference between being truly happy and merely surviving the rigors of life.

Heeding our nudges can also keep us from some rather unpleasant circumstances. My friend, Randie, tells this story.

One Saturday, Randie awoke with a strong nudge to shop for a newer car. This may not seem too unusual, except that Randie hates to shop for cars—doesn't like anything about it. She usually drives one until it stops dead in its tracks! And yet, on this particular morning, the Saturday before Christmas, she jumped out of bed, put on some overalls (no makeup or anything!), and drove over to a used car dealership in her neighborhood. Since she was following a nudge, she hadn't really thought about what she wanted. So, when the salesman asked, she said, "I don't know. Just let me drive them all!"

As she would drive one, he would get another one ready. When she drove the 1996 Grand Prix, Randie, who doesn't even like cars, fell in love with this one! With the help of her husband, she checked the car out, arranged for financing, and purchased it three days later. The next day, they loaded up their children, packed the car full of Christmas presents, and headed for Randie's grandmother's house.

As they were driving toward Lubbock, to her surprise she spotted her old car, the white Taurus she had traded in the previous day, abandoned on the side of the road. Randie reported how grateful she was that God had given her the nudge to buy another car, for she realized that it could have been her and her family, their Christmas presents, and all their luggage stuck there on the side of the road in her old car!

Sometimes not following a nudge can result in a lifetime of sorrow and regret. My friend, Nancy, tells this story.

It was Christmas, 1976, the first year Nancy had lived away from her family. She was en route to her folks' ranch in New Mexico for the holidays. As she was passing through Deming, she had a rather strong nudge to stop and visit her grandfather, whom she hadn't seen in awhile.

Since it had been a long and tiring trip from her home in California, and since she had only 30 more miles to go to complete her trip, she chose to keep on driving, thinking she would go see him the next day. The following morning, before she could get back over to see him, her grandfather died of a sudden heart attack. Nancy has been feeling sorrow and regret ever since.

What stories might you tell? Have you ever been mindful of nudges? What were they like? Did you heed them? If so, what happened as a result? If not, what were the consequences?

As with inklings, recognizing, acknowledging and responding to our nudges also requires the same attitude of trust, sense of expectancy, skill of discernment, and discipline of attention discussed above. And as with inklings, following our nudges takes practice. The more we practice, the more familiar we are with how to do it. The more experience we have following our nudges, the more we will trust them, and the more readily we will respond to them the next time they come.

Because most of us haven't been taught or encouraged to follow our nudges, even more diligence, attention, and courage is required. This is especially true when there are others in our life who have reasons to discourage us from following our nudges. And "reason" may be the operative word here. For as with inklings, nudges aren't "reasonable," mainly because they're not very factual, are hard to document, and thus hard to explain to others. They're also difficult to defend, especially when they evoke fear in others and arouse strong emotions.

What makes them even harder to justify, both to ourselves and to others, is that sometimes they call for extreme and radical responses, which may look to the more rational person as terrifying. In several of the examples cited, persons were "nudged" to change careers, to leave behind lucrative positions that offered sound economic security, and to follow careers that made no such promises. And in at least one example, the person was "nudged" to go against the rules of his job and even risk his own life.

And yet, as noted above, when we do follow our nudges, our life is dramatically, powerfully, and joyfully different. When we don't follow them, we often deny our passion and refuse to claim our calling. Such refusal to respond is far too costly in terms of the nature and quality of our lives. As noted, it can have serious consequences.

To follow our nudges is to follow the Divine Guidance of the God of the Universe. It is to experience freedom as we've never known it before. It is to finally claim our True Self and know the joy and abundance that awaits us all.

Can any of us afford *not* to follow them?

The Call

... The Lord desires intensely that we love him and seek his company.
So much so that from time to time he calls us to draw near to him.

The call comes through words spoken by other good people, or through sermons, or through what is read through books, or through the many things that are heard and by which God calls ...

—Teresa of Avila, *Meditations with Teresa of Avila*

DIRECT DIVINE GUIDANCE

The Third Attempt: Messages

THE THIRD ATTEMPT that God may use to give us the Direct Divine Guidance we need is through what I've called *messages*. These divine messages are not unlike the common, everyday messages with which we're familiar. They come to us generally through one of two forms. They can come to us directly through our own thoughts or through our dreams. Or they can come to us in the same ways as do all messages, through the spoken or written words of others, in all of the various mediums, including conversations, songs, oral readings, written materials, and various audio and visual formats.

And yet, the divine message is like the Word behind the words. It's the Divine Guidance that takes the form of a more familiar message and often goes beyond it to give us a new and perhaps different divine message. And like the other forms of Divine Guidance, these divine messages come to us from the God of the Universe and are intended to give us the information we need to live happy, abundant, productive lives.

Perhaps the only difference between divine messages and all the other messages that we receive daily is their source. In divine messages, the source is not necessarily the one who wrote or spoke the message, but rather the Spirit of God who is seeking to communicate a Word behind those words which can give us the specific information we may need in any given situation to help us best negotiate life and be happy and at peace. Of course, if the Spirit of God so chooses, the spoken or written words of others can themselves be the divine message directly, just as it's given.

However, it's important to note here that the divine message may come through any message from any other source, regardless of the original intention. In other words, God can and often does use the messages of others to communicate a divine message to us, whether or not it was intended by the original speaker or writer.

For example, I've often gotten what I've perceived as divine messages though reading poetry, even, and sometimes especially, through rather racy, earthy, secular poetry that was probably *not* intended to do so. I've gotten them from reading the newspaper, magazines, and novels. I've gotten them from sitcoms on TV and from dialogue in certain movies. I've gotten them from conversations with friends and colleagues. And I've even gotten a few great ones from reading or hearing advertisements.

Compared to inklings and nudges, messages are often more tangible, touchable, and visible. They are often there for us to see and hear, and usually over and over again. We can sometimes read them or share them with others. And because they are usually more present and tangible, we can more readily explain them and defend them to the reticent.

Whereas inklings and nudges are more intuitive, internal, and private, messages are more visual or audible, external and public. Whereas with inklings and nudges, we have to rely on our intuition and feelings, with messages we must now rely more on our ability to listen at a deeper level, more with our heart than our head, and to hear and see beyond the apparent.

To be sure, feelings and intuition are still important here, but on a more secondary level. First, we have to be willing to see and hear what is being said to us in a way that may go beyond the written or spoken word as it's presented, and to go beyond what may have been the original intent of the message. Then we can engage our intuition and feelings to help us incorporate the message into our lives.

For example, as I read some of that racy poetry that I alluded to above, I can, on one level, only let myself hear the raciness of the poetry. I can choose to only take it at face value and go no further. I can choose to be excited and even content with that level of listening.

Or, I can choose to be open to another level, a divine level of listening, using the words of the poetry as a sort of entrée point to enable me to look and listen deeper for another message to me, a divine message pointing me to something I need to hear that will serve as the guidance I need in that particular moment in my life.

The choice to listen to a message at a divine level is

—

quite apparent in a Christian prayer form known as *Lectio Divina*. This particular type of prayer was the normative prayer form for all Christians for the first sixteen hundred years of the history of the church. In recent years, it has seen a revival among some of the faithful.

Lectio Divina means, literally, "divine reading," and as a prayer form it uses scripture as the written or spoken message upon which Christians pray. The process is fairly simple. The ones who are praying read a passage of scripture slowly three times, either silently to themselves or out loud. As they read, they listen for the word or phrase or series of words that may come to them from the reading. Then, they use that word or words as their prayer words, saying them over to themselves quietly, all the while listening at that deeper level for the "still small voice" of God to give them a new and divine message that brings direction to their lives.

The word or words that came to them from the reading served as sort of a "key" to their listening hearts, to open them up so that they could listen at a deeper level and hear the Word from God that could serve as a divine message of guidance for them. The scripture was but the vehicle for the divine word of guidance that they could then use to get healing, direction, or whatever they most needed to live a life of joy and peace.

While Christians traditionally have chosen to use scripture as the vehicle for the Divine Guidance gained through using *Lectio Divina*, other readings could be used. Christians have typically and historically chosen scripture because it is seen as a trustworthy source of Divine Guidance, either on its own or as a vehicle for it within the context of *Lectio Divina*.

And yet, God can and often does use a variety of common messages as vehicles for God's Divine Guidance. As I noted earlier, just about any message, whether written, spoken, or sung, can be used to get a divine message. Our task is to simply acknowledge that God does, indeed, act in this way, and then be expectant and open to the Divine Guidance from wherever it may come.

As I open myself to the possibilities, I never cease to be amazed at the variety of rather common, everyday messages God chooses to use to give me Divine Guidance. One of my favorites is the lyrics to songs, especially country/western songs. I'm not talking about the newer, slicker, cross-over pop country songs. I'm talking about the ones that have to do with old pick-up trucks and fast-moving trains, or that express the kind of love-lost-pain where somebody gets their heart stopped flat, or where some guy's girl just ran off with his best friend, and he sure does miss him. It's the lyrics to *those* kinds of songs that I'm talking about.

And it's through those songs that God sometimes speaks to me the loudest and clearest. Usually it's with regard to the ways I've looked to other people or to various things in my life to be my source of happiness or contentment. And then how disappointed I can be when they don't bring me the peace and fulfillment I'm wanting or needing.

One reason those kinds of country/western songs speak to me is that they tend to address my deepest sadness and heartache, and yet do it in a humorous, even hilarious, way. And because of the humor, I can hear the message and not get defensive. I can open myself to a deeper truth for me, which usually has to do with the realization that only God can finally be my sustaining Source. Nothing or no one else is capable of such a task.

Although messages are much more obvious forms of Divine Guidance than are inklings and nudges, they can be just as easily missed and dismissed. And for many of the same reasons, not the least of which is that, generally speaking, we haven't been taught that they are available. We tend to take a message only at face value. For example, we often believe that a country/western song is just that—a song—something to which we can listen or dance and have fun. It has no other purpose, and surely no other message, especially no other divine message with the purpose of giving us Divine Guidance.

On one level, that may well be true. For the writer and/or singer probably had no other intention in mind, except, of course, to make some money and perhaps gain a little fame! However, to take the stance that a song is *only* a song is but to deny that the God of the Universe can take that song and use those words to speak a Word to us that can give us the Divine Guidance we need to live life fully and with abundance and peace.

Not only does God use spoken or written messages as a way to communicate Divine Guidance to us, but also uses our thoughts and our dreams. In my more quiet moments, when I'm more available and open to listening, thoughts come to me that can only be described as revelations, as direct communications of Divine Guidance, that can point me in new directions, give me new insights to old dilemmas, and provide the Divine Guidance that can offer me exactly what I need in that moment to give me joy and peace.

I've had many such experiences in the midst of my times of meditation and contemplative prayer. I remember one experience that happened as I was leading a group of seminary students in a particular form of meditation. We were to take a word that best described how we were feeling at that moment, put it in a form of a request, and then make our request to God.

As I entered into the silence with the other students, I was aware of how tired I was, and how overextended I felt. This was during an especially low time in my life, when lots of things were not going as I had hoped. I felt as if I was always living my life for others, for their sake and not my own. I felt as if I was always having to prove myself to them, to live up to their expectations, or else suffer their wrath.

In the midst of the silence, which was anything but silent on the inside of my head, I was struggling to put all that I was feeling into a one-word request to God. I was getting more and more frustrated. Then, all at once, I had a vision that Jesus was standing next to me, with his left arm around my shoulders, looking at me, smiling in a most caring way, and slowly shaking his head, as if he couldn't quite believe what he was seeing. Pulling me close to him, he looked into my eyes and said to me in a most loving voice, "Jerry, Jerry, Jerry, don't you know how much I love you!"

In hearing his words, tears came to my eyes, and it all made sense. I had been trying so hard to please everybody else, in hopes of getting their love, all because I had forgotten how much I was loved already. Knowing that I was already loved, I didn't have to try so hard. I could simply relax, love myself, and love them, as Jesus was loving me.

I've also had some rather amazing dreams that have been obvious and powerful sources—messages—of Divine Guidance. I still remember vividly one dream I had almost twenty years ago that not only changed, but may well have *saved*, my life. It had to do with how I was willingly sacrificing my

life and my health for my job, at the expense of myself and
my relationship with my wife and my children. It served to
wake me up and get me on a path of self-care and care for
those whom I loved the most. It made me see that if I did not
attend to those concerns, I would probably not live very long,
and would not be around to enjoy life with my wife and children. Because of its vividness and sheer strength, I paid attention!

Throughout history dreams have been regarded as an important source of divine spiritual guidance. Various ancient
cultures, including the Egyptians, Babylonians, Greeks, and
Romans, all believed dreams to be important ways that human beings received guidance from the spiritual world. In
more recent times, native American Indians have believed
that wisdom came through their dreams.

Modern scholars have continued to explore and put forth
that notion, and many books have been written about the
nature of dreams as sources of Divine Guidance. Two that
come to mind, both by Jungian analyst and Episcopal priest,
John Sanford, are *Dreams: God's Forgotten Language*, and
Dreams and Healing.

When we begin to realize and accept the fact that God
can and does use a variety of common messages to speak to
us a deeper truth, a Word of Divine Guidance, then the possibilities and opportunities are limitless. We become aware
that opportunities for Divine Guidance through messages are
literally everywhere, surrounding us at every moment. This
is especially true in this day and age of mass communication,
in all of its forms, with messages coming at us from all quar-
ters.

Think of an average day in your life. How many messages come to you in the course of a normal day—through the media, from family and friends, through your own thoughts and dreams? I dare say thousands, with millions more available. Each of those common messages can be a source of Divine Guidance for you if you are willing to use them as such. If you are open to the possibility of seeing and hearing them as more than what they appear on the surface. If you are willing to receive them as potential sources of Divine Guidance—guidance that you need and can use to live a happy, abundant life.

The skills needed to receive these divine messages are simple. First, there must be a belief and an acknowledgement that God does indeed seek to address you and give you Divine Guidance through messages, and that this guidance is trustworthy.

Secondly, there must be a willingness to listen at a deeper level, more with your heart than your head. You must be willing to go beyond the tendency to take things only at face value, and to actually set an intention to listen for more, for that Word behind the words, for that message of Divine Guidance.

Thirdly, there must be time set aside to listen, to mediate, to focus on the message so that you may be able to hear what else is being said in it. Sometimes the divine message within the message can be heard very quickly. At other times it may take longer, and more reflection is necessary. Yet, if you set the intention and take the time to get it, then you will!

Those who are so attuned and have the openness and the willingness to get Divine Guidance through messages can become very adept at it. It can become an easy and natural way to get the guidance they need to live happy, peaceful, and abundant lives.

Take Janice, for example. As a very young child, her parents introduced her to books and taught her to read by the time she was four. She found great delight in her reading, both for the sheer pleasure it gave her, and for the information and insights she learned.

Her parents began to notice that when she would share with them about the books she was reading, there was usually something more there than was contained in the reading itself. When they inquired about this "extra" insight or information, she would simply say that it just "came to her" as she read. As they began to encourage her to pay attention to the things that would come to her, Janice became even more attuned to this inner voice. With her parents' encouragement, Janice developed a strong trust in what she was receiving.

As a result, Janice began to rely on her readings to give her guidance in living her life. Now, as an adult, Janice takes for granted that God seeks to guide her through her reading. She expects and trusts the various messages she receives daily, whether it is through books, newspapers, periodicals, or whatever she may be reading. She knows from her own experience that she can get the Divine Guidance she needs by simply being open to these messages, and listening for the Word behind the words. By trusting that Word, she finds that it leads her forth to peace and happiness.

Recently, Janice was considering changing careers. She was uncertain as to just what she wanted to do. Upon the advice of some of her friends, she considered hiring a career counselor and doing some vocational testing to help her with her decision. However, she chose instead to do some meditative reading. She picked some readings that she especially liked, and opened herself to the possibilities of what would come to her as she read. In the course of her readings, she began to get clarity about the career path she wanted to pursue. The more she read, the clearer she got, until finally she was sure of the position she wanted.

The next morning, a friend of hers called to tell her about a new position that was opening up in his company. He had been thinking about whom he might hire to fill this new position and Janice's name had come to mind. It was the same position that Janice had decided upon the night before!

One might say that that was nothing more than coincidence. However, stories like that are not at all uncommon among those who trust messages for the guidance they need to live their life in joy and peace.

Alex told a similar story regarding his search for a relationship. He had been single for almost seven years after his divorce, and was ready for another relationship. He had dated several women, but nothing clicked. He had even searched the internet, and had considered various dating services, but none of that really appealed to him.

As one who had had experience with getting Divine Guidance from messages, he decided to give up his "search" and simply be open to what came to him. Some months later, while watching TV, a public service announcement caught his attention. It was about a local project that needed volunteers. Because he stayed fairly busy with his work and other activities, he didn't normally find time to do volunteer work. And what's more, he didn't feel the least bit drawn to the project. However, each time he saw the announcement, he

117

would hear an inner voice telling him to go check it out. Finally, he got the message!

As he arrived at the volunteer office, he was greeted by a charming woman who interviewed him and explained the opportunity. He was struck not only by her beauty, but also by her commitment to the project. Over the course of the next several months, as they worked together, they got much better acquainted. Now, some three years later, they are married and are expecting their first child.

Cynthia's story is just as dramatic. She had been suffering for years from stress headaches. She had been to doctor after doctor, and had tried nearly every medication available. One Sunday, while reading the church bulletin, she noticed that they were offering a retreat on a contemplative prayer form known as Centering Prayer. The retreat was to offer some basic instruction on the method of the prayer form on Friday evening, and then invite the participants to enter into silence and actually practice the prayer over the next two days.

Normally such events would never have appealed to Cynthia, for she liked neither retreats nor silence. However, over the next several days, seeing the church bulletin lying on the kitchen counter, she was reminded of the retreat. The thought kept coming to her that she really should attend the retreat, though she had no idea why. Finally, on Friday afternoon, much to her surprise, she found herself calling the church office to sign up for the retreat. Three months after learning to do Centering Prayer daily, her stress headaches disappeared.

Jane, like many of us, often looked to her work to find meaning for her life. When it failed to produce, a divine message gave her the courage to make some new decisions. She told me this story.

Jane was employed at a nursing home as a Recreation Therapist, and thoroughly enjoyed her work. It gave her the chance to really get to know the residents, to see them as people of character, with distinct personalities, and not just as old people. Her work went quite well until the beginning of her third year, when her supervisor and another manager began to make her life difficult. They began to criticize her and her work, made untrue accusations, and even suggested that they transfer her to a home in the outback of Colorado. Jane grew clinically depressed as she tried without success to meet their rigorous demands, and found herself crying much of the time.

Then one Sunday, she attended the local United Methodist Church, perhaps out of desperation as much as anything else. In the midst of the service, the choir sang their anthem, with the congregation joining in on one particular verse. The words were from Isaiah, "Surely it is God who saves me; I will trust in him and not be afraid. For the Lord is my stronghold and my sure defense, and he will be my savior."

To Jane, those words came as a divine message, assuring her that with God as her savior, she would prevail, make it through her depression, and be made well again. Heeding that divine message, not only did Jane prevail, she also found another job which gives her great satisfaction, a faith community with whom she shares her life, and a deep spiritual trust in God that she had not known before. She says she has never been happier.

When Luanne was considering marriage, a divine mes-

119

sage changed her life. For nearly 40 years she had waited for the perfect relationship to come along, to get married and have a family. She had attended various relationship seminars, and felt confident that she knew what she wanted.

When Ronald showed up in her life, she was sure she had found the right man. And yet, even with the love that she knew she felt for Ronald, she also felt rushed and hurried as he was advising her to marry him "before football season started" at a high school in West Texas where he worked as band leader. She knew she needed to give him an answer, but was nervous and didn't have peace about it.

In the midst of her indecision, she went to a church close by, found a piano in an empty sanctuary, and started singing and playing classic hymns. She sang several old standards, "Just As I Am" . . ."Amazing Grace" . . . and then the words to another old classic, "Have thine own way Lord . . . hold o'er my being, absolute sway." As she heard those old, familiar words roll off her lips, another thought washed over her— the thought of "giving in " and accepting God's gift of this loving man in her life. In an instant, all fear left her and peace filled her heart as she felt God move in that sanctuary, guiding her to say "Yes" to the marriage that would give her much happiness and joy. They were married less than a month later, and today they share a wonderful family.

Stories like this abound among those who are open to Divine Guidance. We *could* call it coincidence or happenstance or luck or whatever. We could seek to discredit the stories, ignore them, deny them, resist them, or pretend they don't exist.

Or, we could simply acknowledge them and use them to confirm that when we are open to the messages that come our way, and when we trust them to speak to us, then we can get the Divine Guidance we need to live life with joy and peace.

So, if Divine Guidance does come to us through messages, then how might we be better equipped to get and use them?

The answer is similar to that given previously for inklings and nudges. We have to believe that God does, indeed, seek to give us the guidance we need to live happy and abundant lives. And, we have to be open to that guidance in the various forms that it comes.

In the case of the Divine Guidance coming to us through messages, we have to be open to the possibility that there is a divine Word behind the words in the message itself. We have to be willing to listen to everything, whether it be a song, a sermon, a commercial, a poem, or a public service announcement, as if it had a divine Word for us. Then, when those words seem to linger with us, we have to be willing to spend some time in reflection and meditation with that message so that we can "hear" that Word behind the words.

It's been my experience that when a message has a divine Word for me, then quite often that message will hang around, or keep showing up, either in the same form or in various forms. That gives me the clue that there is probably a divine Word there. Then I can choose to spend time reflecting and meditating on that message as I open myself to the divine Word that is seeking to come to me. Sometimes, of course, it will come instantly. Other times, it comes only after reflection and meditation.

Once the divine Word beyond the words has come to me,

---

then I must trust it. I must follow its lead and take the action necessary. Otherwise, I may miss an important bit of guidance that may make a huge difference in my life.

One such missed opportunity came as I was reading the Denver Post newspaper one Sunday afternoon. There was an article about a rather large company in the Denver area that had recently lost several significant contracts and was on the brink of financial ruin. There was an accompanying picture of the CEO. I found myself attracted both to the article and to the woman in the picture, who closely resembled a very dear friend of mine. As I read the rather discouraging facts, the thought kept coming to me to scrape together all I could, even if it meant borrowing money, and invest big in this company. Thinking that I had surely lost all sensibilities, I put the thought out of my mind.

However, over the next couple of weeks, as I would see the article lying on the corner of my desk, the thought would come again—invest big, now! Continuing to resist, I finally threw the article away.

As you may be guessing, I made a huge mistake. For three months later, the CEO secured five new contracts, all much bigger than the ones the company had previously lost, and the stock shot up three hundred percent. If only I had been willing to heed the message to me, I could be basking in the sun on some exotic beach right now!

Have there been times in your life when you have received a divine word through a message? What form did the message take? Did you recognize it and trust it? Did you make use of it? What impact did it have on your life?

Or did you let "reason" cause you to disregard it, as I did

in the situation above? If there's one thing I've witnessed over the last several years, it's that the Spirit's guidance is rarely reasonable. It rarely makes sense, at least as most of us think it should. Facts and reason don't always reveal the truth. For truth is most often revealed only in the Word beyond the words.

When and as messages come to us, we have a choice. We can receive them as if they were only one-dimensional, as if the words of the presented form, as poem, song, article, conversation, or news bulletin, contained the only meaning available, and thus miss the divine message that may be there for us. We can listen with only the ears of our intellect or reason, trusting only in the facts, and disregard the message. Or we can choose to listen at a deeper level, more with our heart than our head, and hear the Word of Divine Guidance from the One who offers us the joy and abundance of a life lived in freedom and peace.

Heeding the messages, hearing the Word behind the words, and acting on that truth can be very beneficial. I can assure you that if *I* had heeded the truth, I'd be on that beach right now!

As you receive the various messages that come to you today, be open to the possibility that there may be more for you there than meets the eye. Let yourself listen, not so much with the rational part of your being, but rather with your heart. Expect the Source of Divine Guidance to give to you through those messages just what you may need to live your life in joy, abundance, and peace. For the Spirit of Divine Guidance is yearning, with sighs too deep for words, for you to listen, to hear, and to follow—and know Life lived in such peace!

123

As you make use of the Divine Guidance that is presented to you through messages, be ready to stand amazed at how free and easy your life can be. For as a Precious Child of God, you deserve nothing less!

Those lacking in understanding may say,
"There is no Divine Presence."
They have not yet opened their hearts to the Blessed One,
to the Beloved who dwells within.

The Holy Spirit seeks out hearts that have been broken,
Ever ready to bless them with strength and new life.

Even when a heart remains closed, seeking its own will,
The Beloved waits with abiding courtesy to hear the
inward call.
Psalm 53, *Psalms for Praying*

PART THREE

Divine Guidance Through the Consequences

Whenever we, for whatever reason, haven't made use of God's direct Divine Guidance, but have depended instead on our own limited knowledge, resources, and ingenuity to get the information we think we need to live our lives, we usually wind up facing the inevitable consequences. These consequences can include being confronted yet again with another lesson to learn, another problem to solve, or another crisis that we hope we can live through as unscathed as possible.

These various consequences are often simply the inevitable result of not using the direct Divine Guidance provided. In other words, when we don't use the direct guidance God makes available to us, and rely instead on ourselves and our own limited abilities to get the information we think we need to live our lives, we can, and with some frequency, wind up having to deal with the consequent difficulties—the lessons, problems, and crises—that arise.

Note here, and I want to be very clear, that God does not *cause* these consequences as some sort of punishment for our lack of response to God's guidance. They are simply the natural results of our not making use of God's direct guidance. Another way to put it is that we most often bring these things upon ourselves because we have relied only on our own limited intellect, energies, and resources to negotiate our life. And, as noted earlier, this can happen even when we *think* we are relying on God's guidance, but in fact are really relying on ourselves to make things happen.

While God, out of God's unending love for us, does not cause these consequences, neither does God give up on us when we fail to make use of the Divine Guidance, and we then find ourselves in the midst of one of the consequences. On the contrary, God seeks to address us where we are, even in the midst of them. Without judgment, condemnation, or retribution of any sort, God works through these consequences as God continues to provide the guidance we need to get back on track and live our lives peacefully in joy and abundance.

In Part Three, I will describe and demonstrate how God can be present in and even make use of those natural consequences—the lessons, problems, and crises—that usually follow our not making use of the direct guidance. And I will show how, in fact, these consequences can serve to wake us up so that God can then have our full and undivided attention as God continues to give us the Divine Guidance that can pull us out of these consequences and allow us to live life joyfully and in peace.

In each of the three chapters that follow, I will describe a particular consequence and how it usually comes about. I will describe its effects and possible resultant outcomes if we don't seek out its cause and it goes unchecked. And I will explore how the consequence could and probably would have been avoided if we had made use of the direct guidance earlier on.

I will share real-life stories from friends, colleagues, and acquaintances that illustrate the particular consequence—the lesson, the problem, the crisis—that comes about by failing to use, for whatever reason, God's direct attempts at giving Divine Guidance. The stories will also demonstrate how God makes use of those consequences as God continues to give the Divine Guidance needed to live a joyful, peaceful life. And the stories will further demonstrate how as one comes to make use of the Divine Guidance, he or she can avoid such consequences in the future, and live the life of joy and peace to which God is leading them.

Then, I will invite you to reflect on the times in your life when you had to deal with and suffer through these kinds of consequences. I will ask you to consider how you might have avoided them if you had had, or, better put, if you had been aware of and made use of, the Divine Guidance available to you. And finally, I will illustrate how God seeks to work through those consequences to still give you the guidance you can use to get back on track and know the joy and peace of a divinely guided life.

All along the way, I will seek to convince you still further that there *is* a better way to live your life—a way far more joyful and peaceful—than having to face and deal with these insufferable consequences for the rest of your life!

129

It is never God's intention that you suffer through lessons, problems, and crises. Rather, when they do occur, God will make use of those occasions to approach you when you just might be at your most attentive and awakened state, as God continues to give you the Divine Guidance you need in order to pull yourself out of those situations and have a shot at a far more peaceful and enjoyable life.

The point here is that God wants and intends for you to know the joy, abundance, and peace of a divinely guided life. And God will not cease until you get it!

O my Beloved, though I have turned from You,
Continue to enfold me with your love;
Be gracious to me, Heart of my of heart, for I am sad and
weary.
Surround me with you healing Light,
That my body, mind, and soul might heal.
Psalm 6, *Psalms for Praying*

DIVINE GUIDANCE THROUGH THE CONSEQUENCES

The Fourth Attempt: Through Lessons

WHILE GOD IS constantly providing the Divine Guidance we need to live a joyful and abundant life with ease and peace, we often, for various reasons, don't make use of it. Instead, we rely on our own limited wisdom, energies, and resources to negotiate our life. When those are not enough, we may wind up dealing with one of the resultant, and often recurring, consequences.

The good news for us is that while we might have missed the various sources of Divine Guidance that have come to us directly, and wound up dealing with one of the resultant consequences, God has not given up on us. Rather, God meets us where we are, in the midst of our consequence, and still seeks to give us the guidance we need. In fact, God often makes use of the consequence and the suffering we may be feeling to wake us up to the subsequent guidance that God has for us. In other words, when we fail to get the guidance directly, then God makes it available indirectly, through the consequence itself.

One common consequence is that of a lesson. While the notion of a lesson can conjure up various types, the kind I'm referring to here has to do with something you generally learn, or at least *think* you have learned, by study or experience, that you believe will help you negotiate your life. To be more specific, I'm talking about what are often referred to as life lessons.

As each of us grows and matures from infancy to adulthood, we learn a number of life lessons. We learn how to walk, talk, feed and dress ourselves, read, relate to others, make choices, support ourselves through some profession or vocation, and the list goes on and on.

Many of these lessons are learned, basically, once and for all, even though we may get better at each one with increased experience. Others, it seems, are not. We learn them, or at least *think* we do, only to discover that when confronted with another similar situation, when that lesson could have been useful, we must confront and attempt to learn that same lesson again, usually through some rather hard-fought experience. And sometimes, we must "learn it" over and over again, *ad infinitum*!

Whenever we get ourselves caught up in such a repetitive lesson-learning cycle, we can find ourselves frustrated, even to the point of exasperation. We can feel confused and puzzled as to why we keep having to deal with the same lesson over and over again. And after awhile, we may start to feel stupid and inadequate, as if we're going brain-dead or at least senile!

We may begin to realize that our need to learn the lesson over again in each encounter can take a huge toll on us as we make the same mistakes over and over again. You may find yourself saying, "If only I could have remembered the lesson learned earlier, I wouldn't have to be suffering these consequences."

Perhaps an example can help bring some clarity here. I have a friend, let's call her Susan, who has had a series of abusive relationships with men. After each break-up, she is convinced that this time she has learned her lesson. She is absolutely certain that she will never get herself into another relationship with an abusive man in which she winds up becoming the victim. And yet, she does. And then, much to her chagrin, she has to learn, yet again, her lesson!

What's going on here? Is Susan a slow learner? Does she like the inevitable abuse? Does she have trouble with short-term memory loss? Is she just plain stupid?

After lengthy conversations with her, I'm convinced she's none of those things. Rather, she's bright, intelligent, and has most of what it takes to have a healthy relationship. Note, I said *most* of what it takes.

The one critical thing she *doesn't* have is the ability to read, trust, and act on the Divine Guidance available to her. Rather, she relies only on her own, admittedly limited, resources. And thus she winds up having to suffer the inevitable consequences, which include not only the series of abu-

135

sive relationships, but of also having to learn the lesson over and over again.

How do I know this? Because I've asked her some critical questions that have given me the information necessary to draw such conclusions. For example, I've asked her if, when she finds herself attracted to one of these men, she has ever been conscious of any even slight awarenesses that hinted that this man was not for her. She said that in every case she had had fleeting thoughts to shy away from this one. And yet, in each instance she had concluded that, given her track record, her thoughts had to do with normal fears of trying it again.

She went on to say that in response to a couple of the men, she had had fairly strong thoughts that urged her to not pursue the relationship. Sometimes it was something he had said in casual conversation, a gesture, or a look. Other times, the thoughts would come through something she was reading, or a song she heard playing.

Again, she chose to pay no attention to the thoughts, passing them off as her usual fear of entering into another relationship. Besides, with each new relationship, she was convinced that because she had already learned her lesson, she couldn't possibly make the same mistake again!

Because Susan wasn't aware of the availability of Divine Guidance, she never considered, nor had any way to know, that these thoughts might have been instances of Divine Guidance. She had no way to know that they might have been God's attempts, through inklings, nudges, and messages, to give her the Divine Guidance she needed to avoid another catastrophe, and having to learn, yet again, the same old lesson.

———

I want to point out here that such "lessons" are not really true life-lessons after all. For they simply don't teach us what we need to know. If anything, they only point out what we still *don't* know and really *need* to know to successfully negotiate life.

In our example, when Susan would manage to finally get herself out of one of her abusive relationships and think that she had once again learned her lesson, all she had really learned was not to get into a relationship with *that* guy again. She hadn't learned a thing about not getting into another abusive relationship, as evidenced by the fact that she again would do just that, get into yet one more similar relationship. Then she would wonder how it had happened! And then proceed to beat herself up for not remembering the former "lesson" she *thought* she had learned.

At this point I think I can hear the wheels turning in your head. You're probably thinking that what Susan really needs is some rather intensive therapy to help her understand the reasons behind why she gets herself into such destructive relationships. Such therapy, you say, would enable her to get the knowledge and insights that would help insure that she doesn't do that again.

I grant you that oftentimes therapy can and does help people like Susan, although it may take several years and cost thousands of dollars. I grant further that that is one viable way to go. In fact, I can give personal testimony to it, both as one who has had therapy, and as one who, as a licensed therapist, has seen it work with my clients. Therapy can be very useful, especially with those who have suffered much trauma and abuse or who have a serious mental illness.

What I'm proposing here, though, is that for most people,

Susan included, there *is* another way, one which does not require years of rigorous and expensive therapy, and can be used by anyone, at any time. All that's necessary is the willingness to recognize, trust, and use the Divine Guidance that's always available.

In our example, what if Susan had known about and had chosen to trust the various bits of Divine Guidance that had come to her? What if she had recognized, trusted, and made use of the inklings, nudges, and messages of which she was obviously, by her own admission, aware? What difference would following the Divine Guidance have made?

The answers seem obvious. Susan would have known and could have chosen not to get into relationships with the particular men with whom she did. She would have known they were not right for her. She would not have had to keep making the same mistakes and then "learning" the same lessons over and over again. She wouldn't have had to go through the self-doubt of her own sanity because she couldn't seem to learn the lessons. And, perhaps most importantly, she would not have had to endure the abuse she suffered.

Our example is but one illustration of what can happen to us when we don't utilize the Divine Guidance that is available to us. We can find ourselves making the same mistakes over and over again, with all the suffering and pain that they bring. And we can find ourselves "learning" over and over again the "lessons" that aren't really learned life lessons at all.

And yet, the good news for Susan, and for any of us, who continues to ignore the Divine Guidance and has to confront the same lessons over and over again, is that God does not give up on us. Rather, God keeps sending the guidance until we are able to get it. And with divine patience, God will make use of the consequence, in this case, the lesson, to get our attention so that we can finally be aware of God's Divine Guidance and begin to make use of it.

Sometimes, it happens like this. We simply grow weary of having to deal with the same lessons over and over again and are ready for something else—for some help beyond ourselves. It may be only then that we are able to hear, receive, and make use of the Divine Guidance.

Such was the case with Susan. In subsequent conversations with her, she has noted that because she had grown tired of repeating the same mistakes and "learning" the same "lessons," she is much more willing to acknowledge and follow the inklings, nudges, and messages that come to her and to see them as sources of Divine Guidance. As a result of her new decision, she is also able to utilize the Divine Guidance in various other areas of her life as well. And she's now able to know a joy and peace that she didn't know before.

All this has happened for Susan because God didn't give up on her. Rather, God met her where she was and worked through her lessons to wake her up to the Divine Guidance God had for her.

Gerard had a similar experience with repetitive lesson-learning. Straight out of college, he had been offered a position in the manager training program with a large department store chain. While the training program was a struggle for Gerard, he was not a quitter, so he kept after it.

His hard work and sheer determination paid off, for at the end of the program he was rewarded with an assistant manager's position at one of the company's larger stores. He liked his boss, and found favor with him, although he did find it difficult to manage other people in his department.

His boss saw his struggles and, out of care for him, encouraged him all the more. Convinced that Gerard did have potential, he sent him to training classes, and spent time personally mentoring him in the skills of being a good manager. Even with all the special attention, Gerard still found it hard to relate to others as their supervisor and manager. He found himself in conflicts that he knew his boss could have handled easily.

Each time, upon reflection, Gerard knew that this time he had learned his lesson about getting into conflicts with those he supervised. And each time he would conclude that because he had learned his lesson, he would not get himself into such situations again. Yet, he would, time and time again. And each time, he would conclude again that *this* time he had learned his lesson.

Even with his supervisor's encouragement, his personal mentoring, and his patience; as well as Gerard's own persistence, it just wasn't working in his present position, at least for Gerard. So, he chose to resign, thinking that perhaps a change in companies might help.

With a letter of recommendation from his boss, Gerard applied for a manager's position at another company. He got the job, and this time thought it just might work. Those whom he supervised seemed happy to have him there, and Gerard found himself settling into his managerial role.

The first couple of months went fairly smoothly. Then, halfway into his third month, the old conflicts started to occur. And as before, each time they did, upon reflection, Gerard would conclude that this time he had learned his lesson, and that no more conflicts would occur.

But, as you may be guessing, they did. And Gerard grew more and more frustrated with himself. He kept wondering why he couldn't seem to learn and remember the lessons that would keep such conflicts from occurring.

Over the next several years, Gerard changed management positions a number of times, each time thinking that this time, in a new setting, with different people, it would be different. And yet, with each change came the same old conflicts, and the same lessons to be learned one more time.

By the time I met Gerard, he was getting desperate. He was beginning to conclude that he was a failure as a manager, and possibly a very slow learner! He was also starting to be aware that perhaps there was something he was missing.

As I visited with Gerard, I asked him if he envisioned himself to be a manager, if it truly felt right. Rather than answer my question directly, he began to explain. He said that that was what he had been trained to do. He had had years of experience in it. And in spite of the various conflicts through the years, he had generally been able to do his job. He did indicate, finally, that it had never really felt like a fit for him, but since he had been trained to be a manager, and hadn't known what else to do, he kept pursuing it.

I pressed further. I asked him if he was ever aware of any passing thoughts when he entered a new job, thoughts that might have felt like cautions or even warnings not to take the job. He indicated that on several occasions he had had such thoughts, but he always dismissed them as passing fears

141

about entering a new job, wondering if he would make the same mistakes in this new job as he had in the last.

He remembered one occasion, especially, when he had had some rather strong feelings that he should not take the job. They came in the midst of the interview, and again he simply dismissed them as fear.

In further conversations with Gerard, it became clear that Gerard had never really wanted to get into management. He had never felt comfortable managing or supervising other peoples' work. He indicated that he had much rather work alone, doing his own work, than to manage others in their work. The management job just happened to be the first position he had been offered after college. And then, once he was in it, he simply followed the path before him.

As with Susan, because Gerard had not known about Divine Guidance, he had never been able to avail himself of it. Rather, he dismissed the inklings and nudges as fear. As a result, he had spent much of his adult life in a career path that didn't fit. He had suffered the humiliation of numerous conflicts that came as a result of not being suited for, or even interested in, being a manager. And he had been confronted over and over again with the same old "lessons," and yet never, ever, really learned them.

However, now, precisely because of having suffered through all the repetitive and painful lessons, Gerard was receptive to another avenue. As I shared with him the notion of Divine Guidance, he was now open to the possibility. He was ready to consider such guidance—guidance that would serve him well, not only in his career choice, but in all areas of his life.

As with Susan, because of God's persistence, God was able to make use of the repetitive lessons to break through to Gerard so that he was open to another way. And Gerard's life and his approach to negotiating it was literally changed forever.

In my work as a career coach, I've encountered hundreds of men and women like Gerard who had gotten into careers that didn't suit their personalities or their gifts. Like Gerard, they had stayed in those jobs for a number of similar reasons, even though they weren't satisfied. And as with Gerard, they had been given Divine Guidance all along which was intended to enable them to make other choices. Yet, because they weren't aware of the Divine Guidance that was being made available to them, they didn't recognize it when it came. And they suffered the consequences—sometimes over and over again, usually to the point of desperation—until finally some were open to other avenues. And because God did not give up on them, or quit sending the guidance, some were able to receive it.

Margo's story is a similar one. Like both Gerard and Susan, Margo had gotten into situations where she had had to encounter the same lessons over and over again. In her case, it was with regards to her rather troubled relationship with her teenage son.

Finally Margo got tired of dealing with the same painful circumstances and confronting the same repetitive lessons. So tired that one day, out of complete frustration, she cried out, "There's just got to be a better way!" That simple cry—that most basic prayer—for help opened her to the guidance God had for her.

As she sat in the middle of her living room floor sobbing,

she heard the sounds of a neighbor's child playing and singing out on the front walk. As she listened to the child's song,
she had the keen awareness, an inner knowing, of what she
needed to do. She rushed upstairs to her son's room, found
him sitting at his desk, and threw her arms around him, telling him how much she loved him. She told him how sorry she
was for not trusting him, and went on to explain that her lack
of trust had come from her own fears of losing him. She then
pledged that from that day forward she would trust him completely as she remembered her love for him.

Because Margo had reached the end of her rope, and had
exhausted her own resources, she was finally willing to acknowledge her need for help. That acknowledgement—that
admittance that her way wasn't working—enabled her to be
open and to "listen." As a result, the Divine Guidance that
she had needed all along, and which had always been there,
was heard. It had come as a divine message through the words
of a child's song that sparked within her an inner knowing.
And because of that divine message, Margo was able to be
reunited in love with her son.

As Margo reflected on that life-changing event, she realized that there had been other times when she had gotten
such messages, messages which she now realized had been
God's Divine Guidance. But out of fear, and even ignorance,
she had ignored them. It was only when she couldn't take the
pain anymore that she was willing to cry out for help and hear
God's response.

Her story illustrates that even when we find ourselves
suffering the consequences of missing the Divine Guidance
that has been made available to us, God, out of God's persistent love for us, doesn't give up. Rather, God waits patiently

for an opportunity—for that moment when we acknowledge that we need help—and are willing to listen for an answer.

As with Margo, sometimes that opportunity is precisely when we are at our wit's end. When we finally realize and admit that we can't do it on our own. When "learning" the lesson one more time is not going to do any good, for we never seem to really learn it anyway. It's then that we have our best chance to hear and trust and act.

Margo's relationship with her son was healed as a result of a divine message that came through the words of a child's song. God's persistence in giving the Divine Guidance, and Margo's willingness to listen, trust it, and act on it was all it took.

Anna's lessons came as the result of her repetitive romantic involvement with a man in her office. She and he had come together and had broken up more times than she could count. The cycle went something like this. He would romance her for a while, take her to lovely dinners, buy her nice gifts, and say all the right things, including that he loved her. She would fall once again for his romance, and take him back one more time.

Then, after a few weeks, he would stop all his romantic tactics, get caught up in his work, pay little attention to her except when he wanted sex, and would, in general, become rather distant. Anna would become frustrated and angry with him, lay down a few ultimatums that never worked, and would then break up with him.

Each time she would come away "smarter" about his ways, having "learned" her lesson. And then, a few weeks later, apparently having forgotten her lesson, as well as his past behavior, she and he would repeat the same cycle.

When she came to me to talk about her situation, she was distraught. She was beginning to question her sanity for "forgetting" her lesson, and for repeating such an unhealthy and unproductive cycle. She was also growing weary of having to confront and "learn" that same lesson over and over again.

As I began to ask her about what would go through her mind each time he would start to woo her back, she was aware that each time she "knew better" than to fall for his tactics. She said she had strong feelings against it every time. She said she'd even had dreams "warning her" not to go back to him. And yet, she concluded that her responses were only her fears of making a commitment to stay in the relationship for the long haul, or her unwillingness to acknowledge that perhaps he had changed.

I asked her to consider the possibility that these feelings and dreams may have been God's Divine Guidance attempting to steer her away from a relationship that would probably never work for her. She was reluctant to believe that this might be the case. And I could sense that this last breakup with him would not be the last. She wasn't ready to hear what I had to suggest.

Several months passed before I saw Anna again. She had just broken up with him yet one more time. Only this time, something was different with her. She wanted to hear again my notions about God's Divine Guidance, for she was at the end of her rope. She couldn't, wouldn't, go through it all again with him. The pain was too great. And besides that, she was sick and tired of the lessons!

As I shared with her, she noted that since our last conversation she had been more aware of her feelings and the dreams, and had become more willing to consider that they may be God's Divine Guidance. In talking with her, I was aware that God had been persistent with her, and had continued to present to her Divine Guidance. God had been able to work through her lessons until the time was right for her to hear.

In hearing, Anna grew more and more willing to believe and to trust the Divine Guidance. She has long since left that relationship, and is making use of God's Divine Guidance in other areas of her life as well. She told me recently that as she now looks back on her life, she can't believe it took her so long to realize that God had been trying all along to lead her to happiness and peace.

Warren's recurring lessons came as a result of his constant struggle with his weight. He had tried every diet in the book, all to no avail. Each time, he came away "knowing" what he had to do—simply eat more fruits and vegetables, and less fatty, fast foods.

And the lesson was clear. If he didn't, he was putting his health, as well as his general quality of life, at risk.

Each time, equipped with reconfirmed knowledge and the lessons just learned, Warren would go to the grocery and stock up on the freshest of vegetables and fruits. And for at least the next couple of weeks, he would do his best to stick to his new diet. Long enough to realize some benefits—some weight loss and a renewed sense of energy.

Then it would happen. He'd oversleep, not have time to pack his lunch, and wind up going out with the office gang to their favorite diner. Rationalizing that just this once wouldn't hurt, he'd order his favorite, a double cheeseburger with extra cheese, a large order of fries, and a chocolate malt—with a slice of hot apple pie a la mode for desert.

Feeling both the exhilaration of his favorite meal and the guilt of backsliding, Warren would begin to waver about sticking to his diet. Soon, he would be back to his old patterns, as the fruits and vegetables grew old in his frig— and his pants grew tighter as his girth grew bigger once again.

Warren didn't like this recurring cycle. He didn't like the way he looked and felt. And he didn't like admitting to himself that he couldn't really learn his lesson.

As we talked one day in my office, I asked him if he was ever aware of any inklings or nudges regarding his behavior. He admitted that every morning as he was getting dressed, he had this urge to pack a healthy lunch for himself, but he let it slide. Then, when lunch time came, since he hadn't brought a lunch, he'd yield to his friends and go with them to the diner.

I invited him to consider that the recurring thoughts he had had about packing a lunch may just be God's Divine Guidance to a healthier life for him. He noted that this was a new thought for him, because he had seen them as but thoughts of guilt, which served only to make him resist all the more. Now, seeing them as God's way of loving and caring for him, he felt a much greater willingness to respond to them.

I saw Warren several months later, and was amazed at what I saw. He had lost about fifty pounds, had more energy than I ever witnessed in him before, and said he felt great.

And he said it was all because he had finally started listening and responding to God's guidance.

Warren concluded that when he began to consider that God wanted a life of health and happiness for him, and was sending him guidance to do just that, he felt motivated to follow the guidance. He no longer felt the same temptation to backslide to his old eating habits, nor did he feel the guilt. He simply followed the guidance to select healthful foods that were both good for him and that he enjoyed. He said it was just that easy!

Warren also noted how good it felt to no longer have to keep learning the same lessons over and over again—lessons that he said he never really felt he had learned anyway. He said it was such a relief to know that God would continue leading him to the life he'd always wanted.

What are the lessons that you seem to be having to "learn" over and over again? In what arenas do they most often appear? Are you surprised when yet again they show their face? Do they shake your confidence in your self? Do you sometimes get irritated that they've come up again for you? Do you wonder why you can't seem to get it, especially when it has come up several times?

When you've been in those situations that have called forth those lessons, have you ever been aware of what you now know could have been aspects of Divine Guidance, such as inklings, nudges, or messages? If so, why didn't you act on them? And if you had, what possible differences could they have made?

And how has God used those repetitive lesson-learning situations to wake you up so that you could then "hear" that still small voice of God seeking to guide you? What difference has it made?

I invite you to consider those situations carefully. Consider their impact on your life. Consider how your life could now be different if you would choose to recognize, trust, and act on the Divine Guidance available to you, at whatever point you become aware of it. What have you got to lose? Except possibly a whole lot of pain, suffering, and hardship, not to mention a great deal of repetitive lesson-learning!

What I'm proposing here is that if you will learn to recognize, pay attention to, trust, and act on the inklings, nudges, and messages that serve as God's direct Divine Guidance, then you can avoid having to try to learn the same lessons over and over again. And furthermore, you can move through whatever reoccurring situations that are provoking the lessons in the first place, and thus avoid the pain and suffering of those situations altogether.

As Susan, Gerard, Margo, Anna, and Warren discovered, there is a better way to negotiate life than by the trial and error of getting ourselves into the same painful situations that then call forth the same repetitive lessons. For the lessons are those that we can never seem to remember and that never finally teach us much of anything anyway.

Learn to acknowledge and use Divine Guidance and you'll avoid those repetitive situations that come about from not being able to remember the "lesson." Use Divine Guidance and avoid the pain and suffering of those situations. Use Divine Guidance, and you'll never have to learn "lessons" again!

And yet, also know this: Even when you ignore, for whatever reason, God's Divine Guidance, and find yourself up to your eyeballs in lessons, God is still there, still sending you the guidance you need. And God will persist and continue to work through those lessons until you're willing to receive the guidance God has for you.

And know this, too: God will not rest until you know the joy and peace God has for you. Of course, for your sake, the sooner, the better!

Hear this, all peoples!
Give ear, all inhabitants of the earth, both low and high,
rich and poor together!
My mouth shall speak wisdom!
The meditations of my heart shall be understanding.
I will incline my ear to the Word;
I will solve my *problems* through the whispers of the Heart's
voice.
Psalm 49, *Psalms for Praying* (italics mine)

Divine Guidance Through
the Consequences

The Fifth Attempt: Through Problems

WHO AMONG US has not had our fair share of problems? No doubt all of us have. And for many, so much so that they have begun to see problems as inevitable and even necessary. What's more, they have begun to see problem *solving* as a necessary way of life.

By problems, what I'm referring to here are those conflicting situations or occasions in which events, people, things, relationships, thoughts, or emotions call for action and some sort of resolution.

Problems of this sort usually cry out for a quick and speedy solution. And depending on a number of factors, not the least of which are our sense of self-esteem, our attitude toward them, and our problem-solving abilities, problems can elicit at least a couple of possible responses. They can energize us and motivate us to solve them. Or they can perplex, vex, and frustrate us, while instilling us with a nagging sense of fear, avoidance, or procrastination.

Regardless of our reaction, problems and our attempts at solving them can tie up a lot of our time, energy, attention, emotions, and reserves as we seek to address them. And, relative to their degree of difficulty or personal importance to us, they can create a high level of stress and cause us a measure of difficulty or pain in our lives.

What I intend here is to reiterate once again and demonstrate further that problems, rather than being a necessary or even natural part of life, are often but a consequence of not making use of the direct Divine Guidance from God. In other words, I want to show again that if we would make use of the direct Divine Guidance that's always made available to us, then we could and would negotiate life in ways that would enable us to avoid most problems altogether.

I will show further that even when we do ignore the Divine Guidance and wind up with a problem, that God does not give up on us, nor does God leave us to solve the problem ourselves. Rather, God takes the opportunity to once again give us the guidance that we can use to both solve the problem at hand and also get back on track so that we don't have to continue to have such problems, and can thus live life with much more joy, ease, and abundance.

Perhaps an example will demonstrate what I mean. Recently a friend, we'll call him Harry, had an important business meeting on Tuesday morning at 8:00 A.M. sharp. It was with two new investors whom he needed for his business, and he wanted to make a good impression. He got to bed at a decent hour, got plenty of rest, arose early, did his morning meditations, ate a healthful breakfast, showered, got dressed, and was out the door in plenty of time to get to his appointment. He got into his car, turned the key, and discovered that his battery was dead—as a doornail. All of a sudden, he had a problem! And immediately, as the gravity of the situation settled in on him, his anxieties began to rise.

And yet, like most folks who are accustomed to having to deal with problems, Harry got into his problem-solving mode. His first thought was to get one of his neighbors to give him a jump, but then realized that they'd all gone to work. He thought about calling a cab, but knew that in the tiny little town where he lives, they'd never get there on time.

As his notions about how to solve his problem started to dwindle, Harry started kicking himself, because he'd been meaning to have the car checked for weeks. The thought had come to him several times, but he ignored them all. Now, Harry had a serious and embarrassing problem, and not a comfortable solution in sight! If only he had listened and acted on those thoughts.

Oh, I can hear your rebuttals. You're probably saying that my example was far too easy. You're saying that in order to prove my point, I picked an example where the person had had several warnings, and because he simply hadn't acted on them, he wound up with a problem. You're thinking he's an irresponsible derelict, and deserved what he got!

And, to a degree, you're right about my example. I did use one where the person had gotten several warnings—nudges—to have his car checked. And because he didn't act

155

on them, he did wind up with a problem. And yes, because he did not act on the warnings, he did, in one sense, deserve what he got, as but a natural consequence.

However, the degree to which your rebuttals are *not* correct has to do with the fact (yes, *fact*) that such "warnings," which I'm calling forms of God's direct Divine Guidance, the inklings, nudges, and messages, come not just in some rare circumstance, one that I've picked to make my point. Rather, those forms of guidance come to all of us all the time, and like with Harry, we, too, often choose to ignore them. And when we do ignore them, especially when we ignore them long enough, we, like Harry, can wind up with problems.

And yet, even when we do wind up with the consequent problems, as did Harry, we're not left solely to our own knowledge, resources, or where-with-all to solve the problems. For even then God is still seeking to give us the guidance we need to solve the problem at hand and live our life with much less effort, struggle, and stress.

And what's more, oftentimes, the problem can serve as our wake-up call. It can serve as the "alarm" we need to regain consciousness so that we might be more willing to listen the next time around—to "hear" God's still small voice which comes through those inklings, nudges, and messages to give us the guidance we need to help keep us free of such problems in the future, and live our life in joy and peace.

Such was the case with Harry. As his own possible solutions to his problem dwindled quickly, and he found himself sitting there feeling like a dolt for not following the inklings and nudges that had come to him, his wife said to him, "Just call the investors and explain the situation. They'll understand."

Normally, her injunction would have hooked Harry's fears even more, caused him to bristle, and he would have chided his wife for giving him such "naive" advice. But this time, when he heard her words, a peace and sense of calm fell over him. For he heard her words differently, as words of divine import. And he realized that this was, in fact, a good test of his potential investors. For if they did not understand, then perhaps they were not the right partners for him anyway.

Armed with what had now become for him a divine message, Harry called his prospective investors and told them his story. As it turned out, one of their cars had not started either, and they had been trying to reach him to tell him they would be late getting into their office and were going to have to reschedule the meeting anyway.

Because of God's persistence, God was able to use and work through Harry's problem to give him the guidance he needed to not only resolve his problem, but establish a more personal relationship with his new partners. For they all got a good laugh out of the situation, which served to break the ice and take their relationship to a higher level. And because of God's relentlessness in giving Harry Divine Guidance, Harry became much more willing to pay attention to it and make use of it to live his life with a greater sense of ease and peace.

Perhaps some additional real-life stories will provide further evidence.

Jamey had grown tired of living in her efficiency apartment, and wanted something larger. In order to afford the bigger apartment, Jamey knew she would have to find a roommate. While Jamey had lived by herself for the last several years, and really cherished her space and solitude, she thought she was willing to sacrifice those things in order to have more room.

She put an ad in the local paper, soon got several calls, and began the interview process. Several candidates showed promise, and she finally picked one. However, throughout the interviewing, Jamie kept having strong thoughts and feelings that she was making a mistake to move and thus put herself in the position of needing a roommate. And yet, her rational mind kept telling her that she was just feeling the normal fears of change.

At first, things in the new apartment with the new roommate seemed to be going okay. But then Jamey started to miss her quiet time alone. She found that the roommate had habits that annoyed her, even though they were minor. And as the days stretched out, she really missed her old apartment and the quiet and solitude it provided.

She started to browbeat herself for not paying attention to all those thoughts and feelings that warned her not to leave her former apartment. She considered just moving out, and back into her old place.

However, she now had several problems. She had signed a year's lease and couldn't break it, she had made a commitment to her roommate and didn't feel like she wanted to renege, and, besides, her old place was no longer available.

If only Jamie had listened to those inklings and nudges, those bits of Divine Guidance, that could have prevented her situation and kept her from having such problems. She didn't honor or act on them, and she suffered the inevitable consequences.

And yet, all was not lost, because, as I indicated earlier, and which is the real point of this chapter, God doesn't give up on anyone just because they don't get it the first time! Rather, God chooses to use the situation and even the particular consequence, in this case, problems, as the occasion to once again make the offer of Divine Guidance.

In the midst of Jamie's problems, and her awareness that she could have avoided them if she had only paid attention to and acted on the guidance, Jamie had another inkling—another bit of Divine Guidance. This time she had the urge to call a couple of the tenants who lived in similar efficiencies in her former building, whom she had met only casually, and see if they might be interested in making a swap. Although she still felt some resistance, this time she chose to act on the guidance and make the calls. To her amazement, the first person Jamie called was delighted to hear from her, because that very day she had been thinking about moving to a larger place.

Jamie acted quickly to meet with her roommate, discuss the situation, get her concurrence, and set up a meeting with the interested party. The two hit it off immediately, and Jamie was able to make the swap.

This time, because Jamie attended to her inkling, she not only solved her own problems, but helped address the needs of a former neighbor. And, more importantly, she gained faith and experience in how recognizing and acting on the Divine Guidance as it comes can keep her free from future problems.

As with Jamie, Eddie had to come to faith in Divine Guidance the hard way, too, through his own set of problems. It had always been Eddie's dream to own a fly fishing shop in a small town. With the support of his wife and family, he quit his sales job and opened his shop in an old mining town in southwestern Colorado.

As a local shopkeeper, Eddie dealt directly with his customers. While he generally got along well with them, there were times when Eddie would find himself saying things that rubbed some of them the wrong way. Sometimes it would be a joke he would tell, or a comment on politics, or a bit of local gossip he'd heard about someone in town.

What was especially baffling for Eddie was that each time he would start to blurt something out that would wind up being offensive to someone, he would have an inkling or nudge not to do so. And yet, almost without fail, Eddie would pay no attention, and blurt it out anyway. Invariably, he would end up with a problem with one of his customers. Then he'd find himself groveling and groping for words of apology to make things right again.

After noticing that three of his best customers, all of whom Eddie had managed to offend with his comments, were not coming in any longer, Eddie realized he had a real problem on his hands. At this rate, he would lose most of his clientele and soon be out of the fly fishing business.

After Eddie had related his story to me, I shared with him the notion of Divine Guidance. Eddie made a commitment to me that the next time he felt the urge to say something to a customer and was aware of an inkling or nudge that warned against it, he would heed the guidance and refrain from saying it. With practice, Eddie gained trust in the Divine Guidance as it came to him, and has established great relationships with his customers!

Are you getting the idea of how this works? Are you remembering any situations in recent months when you were given similar inklings or nudges or messages—which you may now know were bits of Divine Guidance—and chose rather to ignore them? And do you remember what happened—especially the problems that resulted? And do you now see that if you had chosen to act on the guidance given to you that you would have probably avoided the problems altogether?

And have there been occasions when, because of the rigors of the problems themselves, you began to trust the guidance and make use of it? And when you did, did you then find yourself creating fewer problems?

Perhaps some more stories to add clarity.

Sherylanne owned several rental properties in a small mountain tourist town nearby. Because of high demand and the small town atmosphere, she rarely made use of written rental agreements. Although she kept having thoughts that she should use them, she had always made do without them. Usually this worked out well for all concerned. That is, until Sherylanne would get into her fears about her income, and then decide to raise the rent unexpectedly on her tenants.

Whenever she was about to make such a rash decision, she would have strong feelings against it, and would have the added sense that she should make use of the written agreements. Usually she would pay attention to those feelings, at least to the extent of turning loose of her fears, and leaving the rental rates where they were. On occasion however, she would disregard her feelings, yield to her fears, and jack up the rent. Without exception, her actions would cause huge problems with her tenants, and lots of verbal interchange.

On one occasion, however, the problem really got out of hand and went beyond the usual shouting. Three tenants got so angry, they moved out, leaving three apartments to fill in the dead of winter in a sleepy tourist town.

It was in confronting *that* problem, that Sherylanne remembered the thoughts—sources of Divine Guidance—that she had always had when she did not use the written rental agreements. As she shared her story with me, she finally concluded that the thoughts were intended to convince her to make use of them. Now, she knows that by heeding the guidance, she's not likely to create another such costly problem, even when her fears do arise.

At this point, you may be saying that these stories simply reveal situations in which persons finally came to themselves and made use of common sense to solve their problems. For the solutions were obvious.

I grant you that in hindsight the solutions to their problems do seem obvious. And common sense may well have proved sufficient. And yet, my point here is that if they had made use of Divine Guidance—those inklings, nudges, and messages—in the first place, they would not have created the problems that they then had to try to solve. It was only after they had ignored the Divine Guidance and had to confront the resulting problems that they were able to wake up and deal with them. And then, as ones who were at last awakened, they could finally hear and begin to act on the Divine Guidance as new situations arose so that they wouldn't create and have to suffer through the problems again.

Remember, what we are about here is learning to negotiate life by acknowledging, trusting, and acting on Divine Guidance as it comes to us, so that we don't create problems.

This means that we don't have to suffer the effects of these unnecessary problems, nor waste our time being problem-solvers. It means, simply put, that if we make use of the Divine Guidance at whatever stage that it comes to us, we can live life virtually problem-free!

Oh, now I suspect that I've really stirred you up! For you may be thinking that I've surely over-stepped my bounds this time, with all this stuff about how persons really create their own problems, and how they *could* be living life without them.

I know how you feel—really I do—because for most of my life I've simply accepted problems as a natural part of life, and problem-solving as one of my many responsibilities as a mature and responsible human being. I never knew that I was actually ignoring Divine Guidance, at least not most of the time. Nor did I realize that I was, in fact, actually creating most of my own problems.

I just thought that problems were to be expected, and that it was my task to become the best problem solver that I could. The notion of Divine Guidance, and how it could be used to negotiate life in such a way as to avoid most problems, came as new information to me. And for a good while, I continued to ignore it—and usually suffered the consequences. Now, however, I can say without qualification, that following Divine Guidance works!

So, all I'm asking here is that you just hang in there with me. See this thing to the end. Perhaps give it a try and see for yourself. Let your own experience be your source of judgment.

I realize fully that given our typical worldview and our

163

acceptance of problems as a natural part of life, this information, especially if it's new to you, is not easy to accept. It's to
be expected that you might be feeling skeptical.

Leonard was surely among the most skeptical persons
I've known! He was a mechanic at a local garage where I had
my car serviced. He was fairly good at his craft, and yet
seemed to have a knack for getting himself into problems in
his personal life. Due to his willingness to help and his tender
heart, he would get himself into financial straits by lending
money to friends who always had some get-rich-quick scheme
up their sleeves. Even when their ideas really did seem to
have merit, Leonard would have what he described as a "gut
feeling" that he shouldn't make the investment. And yet, he
would, and then wind up kicking himself for being so gull-
ible.

Periodically, Leonard would come to me for advice. And
yet, whenever I'd attempt to help him see that his "gut feelings" were God's attempts to give him some Divine Guidance to stay away from those investments and avoid the consequent problems, he would just laugh and say something
like, " Oh yeah, right, God is speaking to me!" And then, he
would just shrug and say something like, "Well, God sure
must think I'm a dummy!"

It saddened me to see Leonard get himself into the same
situations and have to deal with the same problems over and
over again. And yet, because he was such a soft touch who
really cared for his friends, and because he couldn't believe
that God would see fit to give him guidance, he was forever
creating and then having to deal repeatedly with the same
problems.

For those like Leonard who find it hard to believe that

God would take note of them and seek to help them personally, believing in and making use of Divine Guidance is especially difficult. Because they don't feel worthy of God's love and attention, they miss the guidance entirely, and thus have to suffer through the consequences. And yet, even in the midst of low self-esteem and unbelief, God remains faithful. To be sure, God isn't giving up on Leonard. God will keep giving him the guidance as long as it takes—until Leonard finally gets it!

In many respects, Thelma was much like Leonard. Because of a rather abusive childhood, she found it very difficult to believe that anyone, much less God, would take note of her. She had always had to fend for herself and make her own way. The few times she had trusted others, because of some rather poor choices, she had wound up getting hurt. So she had decided early on that making her way through life was all up to her.

As capable as Thelma was, there were still times when she could have used some help. And yet, rather than ask, she would try it alone. And as you might expect, she often found herself dealing with some rather daunting problems, such as the time she got audited by the IRS!

The day she got the notice that she was going to be audited, Thelma had the feeling that she should seek some help. In fact, several times throughout the day she had the thought that she should ask her friend, Bob, who had an accounting background, to help her. And yet she didn't feel worthy to call him. Instead, she gathered up her files and went to the audit alone.

In the midst of the audit interview, Thelma grew very nervous. She knew there were questions she wasn't prepared to answer, so she tried to fake it. The auditor picked up on her nervousness and concluded that Thelma was hiding something. So, he pressed harder, which made Thelma all the more nervous *and* suspicious-looking, to the point that the auditor decided to do a full audit for several years prior.

Thelma now had a huge problem, because in her last move she had inadvertently discarded some of her old tax records that were now required. If only she had paid attention to the inklings and nudges that had come to her, she could have probably avoided this huge problem. And yet, because of her poor self-esteem and her disbelief that anyone, much less God, would care to take note of her and help her, she missed the guidance altogether.

Later, I had the opportunity to visit with her about her audit, and the toll it took on her. She said she never wanted to go through something like that again. I saw this as my opening to explore the notion of Divine Guidance. I invited her to consider if those feelings and thoughts she had had to seek help when she first got the notice of the audit could possibly have been bits of Divine Guidance—guidance that might have prevented her audit problems. After reflection, and in hindsight, she was able to see that perhaps she had received Divine Guidance and had simply ignored it.

Even though Thelma had never felt worthy of help from anyone, especially God, she also knew of her dislike of dealing with problems. Her IRS audit made her keenly aware of that! So, because of the severity of some of those problems, she was finally willing to consider the possibility of Divine Guidance. She pledged that she would give them more consideration in the future.

Because God was willing to persist with Thelma and to use the problems she encountered to wake her up, Thelma had another opportunity of seeing the possibilities of Divine Guidance. Armed with those possibilities, Thelma can make use of the guidance and avoid similar problems in the future.

Whereas Leonard and Thelma had been unable to make use of Divine Guidance because they had never felt worthy, there are those who don't follow the guidance because they let others talk them out of it. These others may include family members, friends, or colleagues, all who may mean well, but who themselves don't know about or believe in Divine Guidance.

When Angela was only sixteen, she was aware that whenever she had a decision to make, she would get intuitive feelings that sought to guide her. Most of the times, she simply followed her intuition and made her decisions without consulting any one else. On really important decisions, however, she felt more comfortable getting feedback from others, especially her parents, and particularly when it might have a direct effect on them.

Angela had always been a very good student in school, and was now faced with the decision about college and what she wanted to study. She was leaning toward a degree in fine arts, with an emphasis on music. And her intuition was to pursue it.

When she consulted her father, who was a hard working CPA, he had concerns about her choice. He was afraid she wouldn't be able to make a good income in that field. And besides, knowing how brilliant she was, he felt she would be "wasting" her talents on the arts.

Angela had always trusted her father and respected his advice. She knew he loved her and was wanting only the best for her. And yet, her feelings grew even stronger that she should follow her own course. So, she sought to convince him, and thus revealed to him the "guidance" she felt she was getting to pursue music and the arts. Her father looked at her amused, and began to tease her about hearing "voices". And then he began trying once again to convince her to be "reasonable" and choose something more certain and stable, something that would provide a secure income. He even apologized for teasing her, and continued to try to persuade her to make another choice.

His conversations began to raise doubts in Angela's mind about the "guidance" she believed she had been getting. She began to think that perhaps all the inklings, nudges, and messages were simply the foolish thoughts of a child's mind— fantasies she played out in her head.

Finally, after further discussions with her father, Angela decided that she would follow her father's advice and pursue something more "responsible." She decided to be an attorney, and get her undergraduate degree in accounting.

I encountered Angela ten years after she had established her practice in tax law. By all standards, Angela had a very successful practice and was making lots of money. To her father's delight, she was financially secure. The only downside was that Angela was miserable in her career and felt as if her whole life was one huge problem.

Fortunately for Angela, because of God's persistence, God was able to use that problem to wake her up and move her to action. For it was precisely Angela's awareness of her life as "one huge problem" and God's continued Divine Guidance that gave her the courage to claim her life and pursue her heart's desires.

Angela is now convinced that she will never again allow anyone, even those closest to her, to talk her out of the guidance that comes to her. And now, as she pays attention to the Divine Guidance God is continuing to give to her, she's making the transition to the life that she's always wanted!

Angela's story illustrates how easy it is for us to be talked out of the Divine Guidance that God is using to direct us into the life we love—one that suits us and brings us joy and abundance. It also illustrates the problems that are inevitable when we allow ourselves to be talked out of following that guidance. And yet, it also gives evidence that even when we do ignore it, it's never too late. For God is still there to try once again to guide us to a life of joy and peace.

Ted's story is similar to Angela's, only in his case it was not a family member or even a close personal friend who talked him out of following his guidance. Rather it was a so-called professional authority—his therapist.

Ted's guidance had often come through messages he received in dreams. He had followed their guidance for much of his life without the advice or consult of others, and had always fared fairly well.

On one occasion, in the midst of a therapy session, Ted shared with his therapist feelings he had been having lately that perhaps he should call off his engagement to be married. He noted that he had even mentioned his uncertainty to his fiancé, who thought he was just into his fears of finally making a commitment, and brushed his concerns aside.

It was at that point that Ted shared a dream he had had the night before in which he was sure that he should not go through with the wedding. The therapist listened intently, and then concluded that he thought Ted's fiancé was right. He, too, thought that Ted was just into his fears of making such an important commitment.

He concluded that Ted's dream was a "typical anxiety dream, " and he advised Ted to pay no attention to it. He encouraged Ted to deal with his fears of commitment. Ted trusted his therapist, and for the next several sessions dealt with what the therapist saw as Ted's commitment issue.

I met Ted two years after his wedding, right after he had filed for divorce. He said the marriage hadn't worked from the start, and was upset with himself that he had allowed his therapist to talk him out of following his own sense of guidance.

He noted that later, when he had shared his feelings with his therapist in the midst of the marital strife, the therapist only stuck with his notion that Ted's marital difficulties were simply the result of Ted's never having worked through his commitment issues. Ted's wife, of course, felt the same way.

I felt great compassion for Ted, because most of us tend to put a great deal of faith in those whom we see to be our authority figures. And that faithful reliance is compounded by the fact that we also put so little faith and reliance in the notion of the Divine Guidance that comes to us. With such little support for Divine Guidance, it's very easy for most any of us to be talked out of believing and following it, especially by those in whom we put our trust. And even when the inevitable problems arise, it's easy to be persuaded that they are really due to other concerns.

In Ted's case, no matter what the cause of the marital

problems or the divorce, the fact is that Ted knew, through the Divine Guidance he had received, that he shouldn't go through with the wedding. However, he allowed himself to be persuaded, by an authority figure in whom he trusted, to ignore that guidance. As a result, Ted wound up with a problem of monumental proportions, and several persons suffered.

However, because of God's continued guidance, and because of suffering through this problem, Ted is now convinced as he might never have been before to trust the Divine Guidance. And he has decided that he will never give way to another's authority in trusting the guidance.

Sometimes, while we may be aware of the Divine Guidance, we simply let it pass, and then wind up having to deal with the resulting problem. Martha had a nudge, pushed it aside, and as a result suffered much needless grief.

It happened in the months preceding her marriage. She had ordered a dress and a pair of shoes to wear in her wedding, and upon arrival found that they didn't fit. So, she boxed them up and put the package in her car to take to the post office the next day. Early the next morning, she went on her walk at the lake near her house with her friend, Margaret. As she began her walk, she had a nudge to go back and check to make sure she had locked the car, but let it pass.

It was not until a couple of hours later that she noticed the package was missing from her car. At first, she was extremely upset with herself, both for not following her nudge, and for not locking the car in the first place. In fact, she cried and fretted most of the day.

However, soon she had another nudge—to start sending mental messages to whom ever had taken the package to just "toss the box." As she did so, she felt a sense of release, as well as a feeling of assurance that the package would be found.

At 1:30 P.M., she checked her voice mail and retrieved a message from a man who said that someone had "tossed a box" into the back of his truck. He said that when he first discovered it, he thought it was trash. Then he found the dress, shoes, and packing slip inside with her name on it. After checking with directory assistance, he had gotten her phone number.

Martha went to his house and found the package just as she had packed it, with the exception of a few additional coffee stains on it. As it turned out, the man lived behind a church called the Word of Faith!

As Martha related her story, she noted that if she had only followed her original nudge to go back and lock her car, she could have saved herself much suffering. And yet, God did not give up on her, but rather offered her another nudge— one that came in the midst of her suffering. And this time, because of her suffering at not following the first nudge, she acted on this one, and her response made all the difference!

Sometimes, especially if we're fairly skilled at making use of divine Guidance, we can fool ourselves into thinking we're waiting on God to guide us, but are really just pressing ahead ourselves, and, at best, just wanting and expecting God to bless our actions. Then, we wonder why we wind up with a problem and feel frustrated because God is not responding as we would like.

For example, when I decided to move to Colorado, I thought I wanted to live in Silverton, a tiny mining town in the heart of the San Juans. I had been there several times in the summer, and really like the cool alpine climate. When I traveled there in order to find a place to live, I scoured the town looking for a house to rent. While there were some available, there was only one house that really appealed to me. Unfortunately, the owner was letting a friend live there while the friend refurbished another house he owned. It was an open-ended deal, and the friend was free to stay there as long as he needed. After two months of waiting, I grew more and more frustrated. I was ready to move, and I wanted to be there before the summer was over so I could do some hiking and camping in the area.

After several phone calls to the owner, and even more frustration, I decided it just wasn't going to work out. The next day, I received a call from a friend who knew of a house for rent in Ouray, a delightful little tourist town 25 miles north of Silverton, and even more in the heart of the San Juans. The house turned out to be a lovely large Victorian house right in the middle of town. It was far better than the house in Silverton, and I was thrilled. And, as I found out later, Silverton has very harsh winters and they literally board up the shops until spring, leaving the town looking deserted. I would probably have been lonely and unhappy had I moved to Silverton that first winter.

Upon reflection, I realized that while I *thought* I had been relying on God's guidance as I planned to move to Silverton, I had really been trying to make things happen on my own, and had created a problem that resulted in a great deal of frustration. It was only as I, at my wits end, finally turned loose of my own notions of what I thought *should* happen and allowed God to work that I realized God's Divine Guidance. And that guidance made all the difference in my move to Colorado!

Stories abound as to how God uses our problems to wake us up to the Divine Guidance that is available to us. What are some of yours?

I encourage you to acknowledge them, share them, build your trust in them. As you do, perhaps you will become even more aware of how God is constantly giving you the guidance you need to avoid such problems in the future, and live your life with more joy and ease.

For I suspect you've already had your fair share of problems. Now, enjoy some peace!

It is the Lord who directs a man's steps,
He holds him firm and watches over his path.
Though he may fall, he will not go headlong,
For the Lord grasps him by the hand.

Psalm 37:23, New English Bible © Oxford University
Press and Cambridge University Press 1961, 1970

DIVINE GUIDANCE THROUGH THE CONSEQUENCES

The Sixth Attempt: Through Crises

CRISES—THOSE EMOTIONALLY significant circumstances or events that can bring about a radical change of status in a person's life—can wreak havoc. The very word elicits fear in most of us, especially when the crisis may present the distinct possibility of a highly painful or undesirable outcome. We can live our lives in dread of having to one-day face such a crisis.

While we do try to be careful and avoid them, it seems crises are all too common. All you have to do is read a newspaper or listen to or watch any of the various media, and you can find yourself all but overwhelmed by the number and severity of crises throughout our world. One could get the impression that crises are inevitable, even a necessary part of life. And one could conclude that since they do seem to be inevitable, our task is simply to be better prepared and learn better how to handle them when they do come—so as to not be taken off guard and have our lives shattered by them.

However, the question remains, are crises inevitable? Are they a necessary and expected part of life? Should we be content by becoming proficient in dealing with them, as if that were our only choice?

My intent here is two-fold. First, to further the belief that crises are neither inevitable nor necessary, and that if we will but pay attention to and make use of the Divine Guidance as it comes, then we can avoid most of them altogether. And secondly, to show that even when we don't make use of the guidance and find ourselves neck-deep in a crisis, God can and often does use that situation to bring us to awareness, so that we might realize that God is still there, still offering Divine Guidance that will help us deal with the crisis at hand *and* get back on track in order that we won't have to suffer through them so often in the future.

Is that a groan of resistance I hear? Do I hear you saying, "Oh, come on now, you're being way too simplistic! What about those crises that are beyond our control, or that come out of the blue? How can we avoid those?"

I'll grant you that there are those circumstances and events that *are* beyond our control, like the so-called "acts of God" (a term that I've often wondered was coined by insurance companies to limit their liability!)—like tornados, hurricanes, or floods—events that can cause huge crises in our lives. And there are surely those things that come out of nowhere, like the sudden car crash, that can blind-side us and potentially wreak havoc in our lives.

Yet, what I propose is that even in those circumstances—circumstances that can bring on devastating crises—God is still there and still giving us Divine Guidance. And oftentimes that guidance can help us avoid both the devastating effects that would make the event a crisis for us personally, as well as having to suffer any further crises, too.

I will illustrate, through several real-life stories, that God can and does work through the situations of potential crises, and uses those situations to help us be aware of the continuing guidance that God is making available to us. I will show further that as we get and make use of this guidance, we can better deal with the crises as they come, and perhaps avoid any further ones.

So, have patience my friend, and bear with me. I'll now give some examples that might help bring clarity, and perhaps belief.

Joanne bought an older, fixer-upper house, intending to do much of the cosmetic work herself to save money. According to the inspector, the house was basically in good condition, although both the plumbing and wiring were original, and should eventually be replaced.

Shortly after Joanne moved into the house, and addressed some of the cosmetic concerns, she had thoughts several times that she should go ahead and get bids on both the wiring and the plumbing. She wanted to know how much money she would need, and establish a timeline for those improvements. However, her work picked up about then, and she forgot about getting the bids.

179

Six months after she had moved into the house, she had a rather disturbing dream that her house caught fire due to the faulty wiring and burned to the ground. She awoke in a sweat, and made herself a note to get the bids later that day.

While she had every intention to get the bids that day, she got sidetracked with her work and forgot all about it. A week later, she was awakened at 2:00 A.M. by her smoke alarm. Her house was consumed in flames and she narrowly escaped. The fire chief informed her it had started from the old and faulty wiring in the house.

Joanne's ignoring of the several instances of Divine Guidance had resulted in a costly and terrifying crisis. It had cost her her new home, all her belongings, and nearly her life. However, because of her realization that her crisis could have been avoided if she had only acknowledged and acted on the Divine Guidance as it had come to her, she vowed to pay more attention in the future, and act on it immediately. She later reported several instances where her willingness to act on the Divine Guidance had helped her avoid other crises.

Neil owned a local construction company which erected commercial buildings. In the construction process, he used rather large constructs of scaffolding. Knowing the importance of safety, and realizing the potential liability involved, he was very conscientious about checking on a regular basis the durability of the scaffolding.

Shortly after performing an extensive check of all his scaffolding, he had an inkling to check again one particular section that was in use on a new project. He notified his foreman, and was told that everything had just been checked and that there was no need to check it again. Knowing that, Neil ignored the inkling.

Two days later, he got a call from his foreman that the particular section of scaffolding in question had given way and injured two of his men. This crisis, the result of an inkling gone unheeded, had a profound impact on Neil. He felt a deep sense of remorse, as well as guilt, that he had so easily turned loose of the inkling, an inkling that, if trusted, could have prevented the failure and the subsequent injury of his men.

Moved by such feelings, he vowed that he would never again ignore those fleeting inklings. He would be sensitive to them, trust the guidance they offered, and act on them immediately.

In retrospect, if Neil had followed through with taking action on the inkling, the crisis could have been avoided. And yet, because God was still at work seeking to offer guidance to Neil, even through the crisis, Neil learned in perhaps a much deeper way to trust the inklings. Armed with such conviction, not only will Neil be able to avoid further crises as he follows the guidance, he will also be able to follow the guidance as it comes to him in other areas of his life as well. And, as a result, he will have the opportunity to know much more joy and peace.

Sometimes when we ignore the guidance, it can have lasting effects, both on us and on any others involved. And yet, with patience, God will continue to provide the guidance to bring us back to that place of joy and peace.

Sandlyn was a receptionist for one of the local therapists in town. Obviously, she knew all the patients who came in for therapy, and she had access to their files. While she knew it was both unethical and against the laws of privacy to share any of this information, there were times when, with certain of her friends, she just couldn't help herself. Usually what she shared was fairly harmless, although any sharing of confidential information would be reason enough to get herself fired.

On one occasion, while having a drink with some of her friends, she spotted another friend who had that day come in for therapy. From the files, Sandlyn had noted that the friend, who was married, had reported a recent affair with a rather prominent city official. This bit of gossip was just too juicy to keep to herself. Yet, just as she started to share it with the others, she had a strong nudge to keep quiet. For a few minutes she did keep the information to herself and actually felt relieved. However, the temptation was too persistent, and she finally told her friends.

Much to her surprise, one of those gathered, who was a friend of the woman who had had the affair, burst into tears at the news. She began to cry uncontrollably, and all at once jumped up, ran over to the friend, and shared what she had just heard about her.

Sandlyn sat there terrified at what she had just done. She felt ashamed at her lack of feelings for her friend, and guilt for having divulged confidential information. And she was also aware of the severity of the crisis before her. Not only had she just lost two good friends, but she would surely be fired from her job, and have a very difficult time earning trust again. It would take her years to overcome the effects of this crisis.

In fact, it would take more than five years. And yet, what Sandlyn knows now is not only the invaluable gift of trust, but also the gracious gift of God's Divine Guidance that can help her stay true to herself, and also avoid the crises that may otherwise come her way.

In other words, because God was persistent with Sandlyn, and was able to use Sandlyn's crisis to wake her up to the importance of God's Divine Guidance, Sandlyn now lives her life with integrity, and with much more assurance and peace, free from the temptation of getting herself into such crises again. And she is thankful!

In the first chapter, I noted how I had failed to follow the inklings through which God was seeking to warn me that I shouldn't go through with my wedding. I shared how my failure to heed those inklings had resulted in a marriage rife with much heartache and disappointment, and had ended nineteen years later when finally I grew strong enough to file for divorce.

However, now, some fourteen years later, I'm aware that God was able to use that crisis of a marriage to wake me up to much personal and spiritual growth. As a result of my growth, I'm much more attentive to God, am able to see God as my Source, and, I'm far more willing to follow the Divine Guidance when it comes to me. And also, I've learned that crises are never fun, and should be avoided whenever possible!

Through my various experiences, I'm now more convinced than ever that we can avoid most of life's crises if we will but follow the Divine Guidance as God makes it available to us. And I'm also convinced that even when I don't follow the guidance, God is still there to work through that resulting crisis to offer me again the guidance I need to live my life.

———

Sometimes the ignored guidance—even an inkling—can result in a crisis situation that can be personally life-threatening. Depending on how we respond, our life can hang in the balance.

Candie had a habit of stopping at McDonalds for morning coffee on her way to her office in downtown Dallas. One particular morning, as she was about to enter the restaurant, she had an inkling to turn around quickly and go back to her car. She hesitated for a few moments, but then dismissed the thought as ridiculous and entered anyway. As she approached the counter, she saw the attendants start to react as three masked intruders pushed open the doors to rob the place.

Fortunately, the manager had seen the would-be robbers get out of their car and had already notified the police, who arrived quickly to divert the robbery. Candie escaped unharmed, and yet with the keen awareness of how close she had come to being in potential danger.

Because of her close call, Candie is now much more willing to follow her inklings, even, and perhaps especially, when they seem foolish! She realizes the depth of their importance, and the potential consequences of letting them go unheeded.

Sometimes the Divine Guidance may not come to us directly, but rather through someone close to us. However, it's still up to us to follow its lead, or be vulnerable to suffering the consequences.

Jolene was a member of a women's Bible study that met weekly. One of the similarities among the women was that they all had teenage daughters. On one particular meeting day, Jolene awoke with a strange feeling of worry that a daughter of one of the women in the group, Jolene's closest friend, was going to become pregnant. She had a strong sense, a nudge, that she should share this feeling with her friend, but decided instead to share it as a general concern with all the women in the group. As she shared her concern, the other women responded with reservations that any conversations with their daughters, especially about birth control, would be received as consent. Noting their resistance, Jolene framed her nudge in the form of a shared prayer.

Two years later, the daughter of Jolene's friend became pregnant in her senior year of high school—a crisis that perhaps could have been avoided if Jolene's friend had been willing to heed the nudge shared with her by Jolene. Perhaps she could have had conversations with her daughter that might have opened up better lines of communication that may have helped the daughter avoid getting pregnant.

However, the crisis provided opportunities for subsequent conversations between Jolene and her friend about the notion of Divine Guidance, how to recognize and follow it, and avoid future crises. It also led to similar conversations with the pregnant daughter, as well as with the other women in the group.

As a result of those conversations, all involved are more informed and much more willing to follow the Divine Guidance as it comes to them. And now, as they choose to follow the guidance, they have many more opportunities to know the joy and peace of such a divinely guided life.

Sometimes the crisis comes about through what appear to be natural causes, such as floods, tornadoes, or hurricanes. There seems to be nothing we can do about it. And yet, oftentimes, there is.

185

Robert had lived along the Mississippi river all his life. The river provided his livelihood as a riverboat captain and also elicited some deep-seated feelings of home. He never considered thoughts of moving away from it, even though there *were* the occasional threats of minor flooding.

In the midst of her second pregnancy, Robert's wife began to have some rather strong nudges to move their family further inland. She even had some disturbing dreams about flooding that ravished their home and endangered their children.

She shared her feelings with Robert, but Robert only sought to console her. He suggested that perhaps these feelings were simply coming from her protective maternal instincts arising from her pregnancy. He also reminded her that their area had never suffered any major flooding that would prove dangerous, and that she should just let the feelings go.

Trusting Robert's knowledge and life-long experience with the river, she did as he said. She put the feelings out of her mind and focused on preparing for her new baby.

Less than three weeks later, due to sudden heavy raining further north, the levee near their house gave way and sent an eight-foot wall of water crashing against their home. Though she and their first child barely escaped, the stress was too much, and she lost the unborn child.

Robert, who was away on a trip several hundred miles south, heard the news of the sudden flood and was terrified. He tried to contact his wife, but couldn't get through.

Finally, Robert was able to contact his wife and learned of the loss of their home and all their belongings, the dangerous escape, and the loss of their unborn child. Robert was overcome with grief and heartache. Feelings of deep-seated guilt and remorse raced through him.

If only he had listened to his wife and paid attention to her nudges and messages, the Divine Guidance God was giving to her, their personal tragedy could have been avoided. It would not have prevented the flood, but it would have prevented their own experience of the crisis. They could have sold their home and moved to a protected area long before the flood happened. Then, his wife and child would have been spared their terrifying experience, and they could have looked forward to the birth of their second child.

In talking with Robert several months later, he revealed that that experience of loss had had a profound and lasting effect on him. He confessed again his remorse at not paying attention to his wife's nudges and messages. He said he would do anything if he could have another chance. And he vowed never again to ignore such guidance as it came to him.

"If only . . ." Who among us has not said *that*—after the fact, of course? *If only* Robert had heeded the guidance given his wife, what a different experience they would have had.

And yet, what these stories reveal is that even when we do fail, for whatever reason, to make use of God's Divine Guidance, God can still reach us. God can work in and through the crisis to wake us up, to bring us to awareness of the guidance that is still coming to us. For suffering through the ravishing effects of crises, while sometimes devastating, can motivate us to move past whatever resistances we may feel to acting on the Divine Guidance. And sometimes, precisely because of the first-hand experience of the pain of crises, we are often more willing to take seriously the subsequent guidance, so that we might act on it unfailingly, avoid that pain, avoid further crises, and live our lives in more joy and peace.

While I encourage you to take seriously the Divine Guidance as it comes to you so that you might avoid most of life's crises, I also want you to know that even when you don't, God is still there for you. God is still present, attentive, and still sending to you the guidance necessary for you to move through the crisis and know more of the joy and peace that God has for you.

And while suffering through a crisis can be painful and even devastating, God can use it to impress upon you the importance of following the Divine Guidance as it continues to come to you. Unfortunately for some, it seems that only the pain of a crisis can wake them up to the availability and importance of following God's Divine Guidance.

Be that as it may, God is still there in the midst of it to pull them through and continue to offer guidance. And the sooner they make us of it, the better for all concerned!

How would your life be different if you unceasingly made use of God's Divine Guidance? Would you be less apt to have to confront crises? Would you live life with less fear and more confidence and assurance? Would you know more success and happiness, more joy and peace?

The choice is yours. And believe me, you *are* making that choice every moment of your life, either consciously or unconsciously.

You can ignore or disregard the guidance and continue to take your chances with potential crises for the rest of your life—which really won't offer you much *rest*!

Or you can choose a better way, deciding to follow God's Divine Guidance, and know the life of abundance and ease that God has for you.

Which will it be?

Those who dwell in the shelter of
Infinite Light, who abide in the wings of
Infinite Love,
Will raise their voices in praise:
"My refuge and my strength;
In You alone will I trust."

... For You have sent your angels to watch over me, to
guide me in all my ways.
Psalm 91, *Psalms for Praying*

PART FOUR

A Better Way—the Secret Revealed!

Throughout this book, my intention has been to give to you enough information and more than enough evidence to convince you that you *can* live your life freely and in peace, and that it's as easy and simple as following God's Divine Guidance. I've sought to persuade you that there is no logical, moral, religious, or spiritual reason for you to have to suffer through a lifetime of lessons, problems, or crises. For the fact of the matter is that life is usually only as difficult as we make it.

My hope has been for you to realize and know that there is a far better way for you to live your life than thinking you have to depend only on your own resources and ingenuity to get the information you need to live your life. For when you do that, you can easily find yourself vulnerable, afraid, and invariably suffering the various effects of the resultant consequences.

In this chapter, I will continue to put forth my case for a better way—the way of God's Divine Guidance—and will offer some insights and resources that may prove helpful to you. And I pray that you will come away not only knowing that there *is* a better way, but actually following that better way. For I know that if you do so, you will find this better way far less stressful, chaotic, fearful, and fragile, and your life much more certain, rewarding, joyful, and easy as you trust God to guide you.

May God's Guiding Spirit of Peace be with you as you choose the better way!

This Holy Instant would I give to You.
Be You in charge.
For I would follow You certain that Your direction gives me
peace.
Lesson # 365—*A Course in Miracles*

A BETTER WAY: THE SECRET REVEALED!

THE SECRET TO an abundant life is to be found in this fact: life is only as difficult and deficient as you make it—and as easy and abundant as following God's Divine Guidance. For the truth of the matter is that the nature and quality of the life you live is a choice—your choice. You can choose for it to be difficult and deficient. Or you can choose for it to be easy and abundant. It *is* your choice—and it is determined by how you choose to respond to Divine Guidance.

And whether you realize it or not, you *do* make that choice—every moment of your life—in every decision you make and in every action you take. No one else is responsible, nor to blame, for the life you choose to live and how you choose to live it. That's the good news for you, although it may not seem like good news if you're hoping or wanting someone else to be responsible for your life. The sooner you realize that you are responsible for and in charge of deciding the nature and quality of your life, the sooner you can make a *conscious* choice as to the life you will live, and how you will live it.

Throughout this book I have sought to make the case for what I believe to be a better way to live our lives—a way far easier and more joyful than by having to suffer through learning one more lesson, solving one more problem, and surviving one more crisis. For I take as absolute *fact*—and seriously hope that you do too by now—that the life you live and how you live it is your choice, and that it's as difficult or as easy as you choose to make it.

Based on that reality, I have proposed that if you will choose to follow the Divine Guidance that is constantly made available to you, then your life will be far more peaceful and easy than if you do not. For as you follow God's Divine Guidance, you will be able to avoid many, if not most, of the inevitable consequences—the lessons, problems, and crises—that often come as a result of not following the guidance.

However, as I have also noted throughout this book, to make a conscious choice to follow the Divine Guidance is often not easy. For to be able to make an informed decision, we must have the information necessary—and the skills and courage required to make that decision in the best possible way. Unfortunately, most of us have not known, until now, that Divine Guidance is even available to us, nor have we been taught the tools necessary to receive it. Add to that the distrust that most have for anything that goes beyond the tangible and the reasonable, and it's no wonder that we haven't been able to make a conscious choice to follow Divine Guidance.

Therefore, what I hope to give here is further encouragement for you to do whatever is necessary—whatever it takes—to be able to follow Divine Guidance. For I do want you to know the certainty, the ease, and the peace that it offers you as you make your way through the course of your life.

With that goal in mind, what I offer now are some insights, resources, and tools that can be helpful in assisting you to be able to "hear" and "see" and follow the Divine Guidance as it does come to you. For it is never too late to begin to follow God's Divine Guidance, and know the peace, ease, and abundant life that God intends for you.

Perhaps the most important action we need to take as we are considering the notion of Divine Guidance is to simply *decide* that we are willing to hear, see, trust, and make use of the Divine Guidance as it's made available to us. We must actively set the intention to utilize the Divine Guidance in whatever forms it may come. Setting such an intention will serve us well, especially in those situations when we feel resistance to it. Or in those circumstances when we may start to doubt the guidance because we feel foolish or uncertain.

Constantly setting and resetting our intention on a daily, perhaps even hourly, basis will give us the commitment we may need to hold fast to our decision to follow the Divine Guidance. It will insure that we don't cave in to the old patterns of "overlooking" the guidance, letting it pass as unimportant, or simply disregarding it as it comes to us. It will insure that we don't let anything or anybody keep us from our commitment to ourselves that we will heed and make use of it, so that we can avoid the inevitable consequences, and thus live our life in ease and peace.

Once you have set the intention to receive and make use of Divine Guidance, you may need a tool that will enable you to "hear" the Divine Guidance as it comes to you. Such a tool is usually necessary, because you and I live in a world that is filled with information, animation, and action, and we can find ourselves overwhelmed with sensory overload. It seems that most of the time we're plugged into something— a cell phone, a personal CD player, car stereo, or some other sound-producing gadget—and sometimes we're not even aware of it. I remember being in my car several years ago and having the thought that I'd like to listen to the radio. As I reached to turn it on, I realized that it was already on, blaring away, and I hadn't even noticed!

Surrounded by such sensory overload, quite often our eyes dart from one scene to another, our minds race with thoughts of all kinds, and our hearts try to keep pace with the demands of our bodies. Even when we do turn down the volume on the outward sounds and try to find a quiet place to relax, unwind, and listen, our minds are still going ninety-to-nothing. The internal "noise" and activity are still blaring, ceaselessly, whether we are awake or asleep.

Filled with such unending, persistent, noisy commotions and inner activity, it's no wonder that we can't hear the "still small voice of God" within us—the voice of God's Divine Guidance. Amidst all that internal distraction, we may find ourselves yearning for some quiet, some internal silence that will allow us to hear that guiding voice seeking our attention.

And yet, without some way to quiet the rambling and raging voices in our minds, we may never be able to hear and make use of that guidance. We will be left to fend for ourselves, to make our own way through life, as best we can, with only our own knowledge and resources to guide us. And we'll be left to suffer the inevitable consequences that happen when what we know is not enough.

The tool that has been the most helpful and important to me in enabling me to quiet those distracting voices in my head and be able "hear" the voice of Divine Guidance has been a contemplative prayer practice that I learned several years ago. Although there are numerous forms of contemplative prayer, depending on which religious or spiritual tradition you may prefer, the one I use is called Centering Prayer.

As with most contemplative practices, Centering Prayer gives me a method of turning loose of thoughts as they come through my consciousness. The method is quite simple—as thoughts come, I let them go. As I do so, I am able to rest in the silence. And as I continue to let the thoughts go, and allow that reservoir of deep silence to develop, I am learning, through daily practice, a discipline of detachment.

This discipline of detachment is not a detachment from life or from the world. On the contrary, it is rather a detachment from all the distractions that would keep me from being truly present *to* life, and that would keep me from hearing God's guidance. This discipline of detachment enables me to turn loose of my attachments to the myriad thoughts—to the "noise"—in my head that can keep me distracted and thus unable to be fully present to God's guidance, and to clearly "hear" it when and as it comes.

The reservoir of silence that has been created, combined with the discipline of detachment, allows me to take that experience into my daily life. This is particularly helpful when the noise and distractions of my life start to consume my mind and keep me from hearing God's guidance. When that happens, as often it does in the busyness of life, I can use that

199

discipline to enable me to turn loose of those distractions and remain centered. From that centered place of deep silence, I am better able to "listen" and thus "hear" the Divine Guidance when it comes.

An excellent explanation of Centering Prayer is found in a book written by one of its creators, Father Thomas Keating, entitled *Open Mind, Open Heart: The Contemplative Dimension of the Gospel*. Here Father Keating gives an overview of contemplation, a brief history of contemplative prayer, and a detailed explanation of the method of Centering Prayer. He also addresses common questions that those who practice the prayer may have as they move through the experience. If you are interested in this discipline, I highly recommend this resource.

I can truly say that Centering Prayer has been invaluable to me as I have sought to actively follow God's Divine Guidance in my life. Because of the reservoir of silence that it enables in me, as well as the discipline of detachment from all the distractions, I am far more able to receive the guidance as it comes, and can thus avail myself of its benefits. Therefore, I encourage you to find a contemplative practice that can do the same for you.

Once you have set the intention to receive and make use of Divine Guidance and have found a way to hear it when it comes, you may find it helpful to develop an attitude of expectation—a moment-by-moment attitude of expectancy—that God will provide you with the Divine Guidance you need, when you need it, to help you live your life in peace, ease, and harmony with all of creation. This expectant attitude will instill in you a discipline of watchfulness so that you are constantly watching, waiting, and expecting the guidance to come to you. You will be on the lookout for it, so that it doesn't take you by surprise, or so that you don't miss it when it comes.

This attitude of expectation will also give you reasons to wait upon God rather than think you must plunge ahead with your own notions of direction, limited by your own knowledge and resources, and seek to address the situation in which you find yourself. In other words, it will give you cause to pause and wait upon God and God's Divine Guidance, rather than think it's up to you to jump in there and fix the situation or make the decision. And it will probably give you a great sense of relief, knowing that you can relax as you trust in God to give you the guidance you need to address any situation.

Another related practice, once you have set the intention to follow the guidance and have developed an attitude of expectation, is to dialogue with whatever resistances you may feel to making use of the guidance as it comes. For example, let's say that I'm getting a nudge to have my car checked out, and yet I'm feeling resistance because it's been only a couple of thousand miles since I had it serviced, and it seems to be running fine. Perhaps rather than simply disregarding these resistances and going with my nudge, or ignoring the nudge and trusting my resistances, it would prove helpful if I "spoke" with these resistances to see what they're trying to tell me.

I've actually had this "conversation," and what I discovered was some old "tapes"—stored memories—about not trusting auto mechanics, because, in the past, some of them had ripped me off, charging me for work that didn't need to be done. As I considered this "feedback" from my resistances, I asked myself if I trusted the auto mechanic I presently use. I decided I did, and so ignored the resistance and took my

201

car in for service. Indeed, there was an impending problem, that if addressed immediately would keep me from bigger and more costly repairs down the road, or even from possibly being stranded out on the highway. I was glad I had dialogued with my resistances, for then I could follow the Divine Guidance with more confidence.

Once you have decided to follow your Divine Guidance, do so with gusto! Jump in there with all your trust and might. Follow it with full confidence that God is leading you to a life of peace and ease.

And, as an act of faith and confidence, do whatever you are divinely guided to do. Don't let yourself start to question, change, or modify it on your own. Trust the Divine Guidance precisely as it comes to you. Don't judge it or even expect that it make sense. Take the "risk" that it is just as it is supposed to be—just as God intends it to be. For if you yield to your desire to make changes in the "instructions," for whatever reasons, then the guidance is no longer God's Divine Guidance, but rather simply a version of your own. And you and I both know the dangers of that—those blasted inevitable consequences!

So, just go with the Divine Guidance precisely as it is presented to you, even though it may feel "risky" without your more "rational and reasonable" modifications. You'll be glad you did, for the only thing really "at risk" is avoidance of the consequences. And we've all had enough of those to last us a lifetime!

Also, as you trust the guidance just as it comes to you, you'll have the added benefit of increased confidence in the accuracy of God's Divine Guidance. Such increased confidence will, in turn, make it easier for you to trust it again just as it is presented.

Another thing I find helpful is to actively acknowledge the Divine Guidance as it comes to me. As I acknowledge the Divine Guidance, my experiences help confirm that Divine Guidance really is available to me constantly and in various forms. Armed with personal evidence, I can more readily trust it at subsequent times.

I also find it helpful to note when the guidance doesn't seem to be coming to me, at least not as I expected it or on my time-table. What I've discovered is that I was not really ready for it, at least not like I wanted it. For example, there have been times when I thought I had a certain writing project complete and was ready to decide where I would have it published. As I sought God's guidance to direct me, I was met with confusion and indecision, only to discover as I again looked over the project that there were significant corrections and improvements I needed to make to it before it was really ready for publication. The Divine Guidance, I realized, was in the "not yet." It was present in the midst of my confusion and indecision, pointing me toward what *needed* to be done rather than what *I* thought ought to be done. And, always to my surprise, the guidance had been there all along. I just wasn't recognizing it. For it seems that sometimes the guidance *is* the confusion and indecision, all but forcing me to wait and gain clarity, or, as in the example above, discover further what needed to be done before I was really ready for what I wanted to happen. Afterwards I realized that, in essence, I was not really waiting on God's guidance as much as I was waiting on God to supply what I wanted, when I wanted it.

As a result of those "not yet" experiences, I am much

more willing to see and trust the guidance when it does not *seem* to be there. Now I know there's a reason for my confusion and indecision and what feels like God's non-response, and I'm willing to sit with it until I see what the *real* Divine Guidance is—not simply what I think it ought to be.

After you've built up a personal history of making use of God's Divine Guidance, I encourage you to tell others about it. You may want to begin by just telling a close friend, some one who accepts and trusts you, and can hear and receive what you have to say without judgment. This will help confirm your confidence in the guidance.

Once you've gained sufficient confidence, then spread the word to as many as will listen, especially to those whom you think might be readily open to the idea. The more you talk about it to those who can receive it, the more confidence you will have in it yourself. The more confidence you have in it, the more you will feel inclined to make even more use of it—and the more benefits you will receive.

As you find those who are especially open to the idea, begin to share with them what you have learned about making use of Divine Guidance. Teach them all you know. The notion here is that as you teach what you know, you also learn, at an even deeper level, what you teach. And as you teach, you can also learn from those you teach, for they will have their own insights to share with you.

The more you teach, the more you will know. The more you know, the more confidence you will have, and the easier it will be for you to follow the guidance. Also, as those you teach begin to get it, they will contribute to your increased level of confidence, too.

In addition, the more you teach, the more the information begins to penetrate into your subconscious. Then, as situations arise, and the guidance comes, you may find it even easier to make use of it.

Another helpful tool is to keep a journal of your experiences with Divine Guidance. You might record the situation, how the guidance showed up, and what happened. You might also want to record any feelings that you had as the experience unfolded, noting especially feelings of trust or doubt, exuberance or fear, and how those feelings affected your actions. You may want to record any new insights you've had, or any new decisions you've made.

Be especially mindful of those times when, as a result of not following the Divine Guidance, you found yourself dealing with one of the consequences—the lessons, the problems, or the crises. Record any feelings you had then, any regrets, any new insights. Record any awarenesses you may have had of attempts at previous Divine Guidance that you either overlooked, ignored, or consciously chose not to follow that may have helped you avoid the consequence.

Also, record how you may have seen God at work in the midst of those consequences, perhaps trying to wake you up to the possibilities, still attempting to offer you Divine Guidance. Let your reflections on those experiences help you decide how you want to respond in the future.

Periodically, review your journal, letting it inform you of your progress in following God's Divine Guidance. The information recorded may help you better call to mind and remember those situations in which you either did or did not follow the guidance, and the consequences of each. Your review may provide the "evidence" you need to be much more

205

cognizant of and consistent in recognizing the Divine Guidance in whatever form in which it may be presented to you. And it may prove beneficial in helping you to be even more diligent in following the guidance in future situations.

The memories recorded may help you in that split-second moment as you are deciding whether to follow the guidance or simply dismiss it. And it may be that the recall of those past experiences will give you the courage and insights you need to make an informed, confident decision to follow the guidance rather than let it go.

One awareness that you may have as you keep your journal is the degree to which you might have certain attachments to keeping and maintaining various lessons, problems, and crises in your life. I know it sounds insane (which, basically, it is!) to say that we actually want to keep such difficulties alive and well in our lives. However, the fact of the matter is that sometimes we do. And unless we acknowledge our attachments, we don't have a chance in changing them. And left to their own devices, such difficulties can wreak havoc in our lives.

As you become aware of your attachments to lessons, problems, or crises, you may gain insight as why you want to keep them around. Perhaps having them in your life is a way that you get attention from others. For example, people with lots of problems tend to attract others with problems, who can then spend untold hours commiserating with them. They often join various self-help groups that are formed around shared problems, and also serve to meet social and communal needs as well. Also, they tend to attract those who like to solve problems, who can shower lots of attention on them.

Perhaps your attachments provide ways to be commended

by others. The world loves those who can take a complicated problem and provide an easy solution.

Perhaps they seem like a useful way to structure your time, or give your life a sense of meaning and purpose as you address them. Or perhaps, as I alluded to earlier, they may be at the heart of your vocational or professional life. You may actually find yourself both fiscally and emotionally dependent on them for your livelihood and your sense of personal esteem.

As you review your journal and discover and acknowledge your attachments, you may want to question whether you still desire to hang onto them. You may want to find other ways to meet the needs that they have addressed in yourself. For I suspect you are paying a sizeable price, emotionally, spiritually, and even physically, for keeping them in your life.

Let your journal be as detailed as possible and serve as an ongoing record of Divine Guidance in your life. It can prove helpful as a testimony as to how God has been active in guiding you through the maze of life, especially in those times when it seems that God is not.

If you choose not to keep a journal, then you might find it helpful to simply keep an ongoing list of occasions when you were aware of Divine Guidance. As with a journal, your list can prove helpful to confirm God's guiding presence in your life, and perhaps give you increased confidence in making better use of Divine Guidance.

Once you have built up sufficient "testimonies" of your experiences with Divine Guidance, share them with others. As you share them, you will re-live them, and as you re-live them in the telling, you will be making them even more indelible in your mind.

And be sure to share both kinds of experiences, those in which you followed the guidance, and those in which you didn't. You need to acknowledge and remember both, for both will serve to inform your next decision.

As you share your experiences—your testimonies—invite others to share theirs. You may find yourself pleasantly surprised at how many you hear. And you may find yourself amazed at the depth of experiences that are shared. These shared testimonies will serve to give all concerned further evidence that God is, indeed, at work in our lives personally, to give us the guidance we need to negotiate our lives with ease and peace. And they will add increased confidence that such guidance is neither a fluke nor some sort of rare and extraordinary miracle, but rather an everyday occurrence in the lives of those who are open to it.

As I was writing this book, I invited several friends to share with me their experiences with God's Divine Guidance. Most all of the stories that you have read here came from them.

As I received their testimonies, I found myself feeling very blessed, as well as very excited for my friends, that they were aware of and making use of God's Divine Guidance in their lives. Their stories increased my faith, and gave me even more proof that Divine Guidance is both real and available to us all. And they gave me increased incentive to share all this with you through this book, so that you, too, could know the joy and peace of making use of God's Divine Guidance.

Another important resource that you may find helpful as

you seek to follow Divine Guidance is to gather together others who are willing to follow the guidance. This community of faithful followers of God's Divine Guidance can serve as a great source of strength, encouragement, support, and celebration.

As I've mentioned several times, following Divine Guidance is not easy, especially amidst those who do not understand nor believe in it. Their negative influence can take its toll on us. Therefore, we may need and can surely use a supportive group of others who do understand, and who are willing to join with us in following the guidance.

Perhaps the group would choose to meet regularly to share their experiences. As members begin to relate their personal testimonies, and as each gets more comfortable with the notion of talking about Divine Guidance in the midst of a group, each will also gain confidence and trust in making use of Divine Guidance.

As each of us regularly shares our stories and offers support and encouragement to one another, we each gain strength and insight into the various ways we can continue to follow the guidance. Armed with such conviction, we can claim courage and stand firm when confronted by those who don't understand or believe, and who would seek to discourage us.

Perhaps this book can serve as a resource that you and your group can read and study together. As you share together what each gets from the book, new ideas will surely emerge that may prove helpful to all.

As you become more at home with using Divine Guidance and with sharing your experiences, you may want to offer the book to others, especially to those whom you see to

209

be receptive. Perhaps you can use it as a way to introduce the subject and begin the conversation with them.

Spreading the word about God's Divine Guidance is extremely important, because as more and more people are exposed to the notion of Divine Guidance, the easier it is for all of us to encourage each other to make use of it. The more we all make use of it, the more peace and harmony there will be, not only in our lives, personally, but throughout the entire world. And that's a worthy goal for us all!

The last insight and encouragement I offer is the notion of giving thanks. I find it very important to give thanks to the One who constantly makes Divine Guidance available to me. Such an attitude of gratitude can do much to keep me mindful of all the ways God has sought to offer me the particular Divine Guidance I needed at just the right time to best negotiate my life. It gives me an opportunity to remember and to recognize again the constant nature of that guidance, and to realize with increased confidence that the guidance will always continue.

Being thankful also keeps me attentive to and expectant of Divine Guidance in all the ways it may appear in my life so that I'm not nearly as likely to miss it when it comes. And I find that the more I express my thankfulness, the more conscious I am of even more Divine Guidance for which I can be thankful.

As you follow God's Divine Guidance, you may become aware of other important tools or insights that are helpful to you. For the fact of the matter is that when you are ready and willing to receive God's Divine Guidance, then God will give to you what you need to be able to follow it. As you do your part of setting that intention, then God will do God's part of providing whatever it takes to enable you to receive and follow God's guidance.

Given that, it's now up to you. The secret is out, and it's your decision. Are you ready for a better, more joyful, more peaceful way to live your life? Are you ready to give up whatever attachments you may have to lessons, problems, and crises in your life, and let God meet those needs in other, more gratifying, satisfying, and edifying ways? Are you willing to set the intention and to equip yourself to follow the Divine Guidance as it comes to you?

Simply put, the question is this: Are you ready and willing to follow God's Divine Guidance and know the Life that God has for you?

I pray that you are. For, indeed, a life of peace, joy, and abundance awaits you if you will.

And, my Beloved Friend, as a Precious Child of God, you deserve nothing less!

Let me know how it goes. And Godspeed!

211

Printed in the United States
1136200002B/142

9 781401 031060